Cheetahs can sprint at shocking speeds of nearly **60 miles an hour!** (96.6 km/h)

NATIONAL
GEOGRAPHIC
KiDS

WASHINGTON, D.C.

What is an INFOGRAPHIC?
And what's this book ALL ABOUT?

You probably see numbers every day, but there aren't just ordinary numbers in this book! *By the Numbers 2.0* is all about bringing data to life so you can understand the story behind the figures. Say goodbye to boring old numbers listed on the page. Instead, you'll see them in amazing photos, cool illustrations, fascinating graphs, and wacky charts. How'd we do it? Welcome to the world of infographics!

These *information graphics* combine the powers of design and data to show sometimes confusing numbers in a quick, fun, and uncomplicated way. Infographics come in a bunch of different shapes, sizes, patterns, and colors, and you'll find them all in this book. So get ready to be amazed, surprised, and completely captivated. You're about to see numbers, data, and statistics like you've never seen them before.

Infographics in this book:

PHOTO INFOGRAPHICS
Beautiful photos are used in a photo infographic to illustrate numbers and data, while pop-outs present the facts behind the figures. See pages 44–45 and 220–221.

WORD CLOUDS
A word cloud is exactly like how it sounds—a cloud of words, in which each word's size varies. Word clouds represent the concept of frequency in math and statistics—the bigger the number, the more important it is. See pages 16–17.

MAPS
When a location is involved, it's helpful to see the data plotted out on a map of the country— or even the world! Look for location markers to help you find specific data points on each map. See pages 142–143.

PIE CHARTS

Surely you've seen a pie before. Imagine it split up into slices, with each section representing a specific percentage of the whole. Voilà! You've got yourself a pie chart. See pages 54–55 and 114–115.

VISUAL ARTICLES

Have you ever read something that seems too confusing to grasp? That's when visual articles are most useful. These are infographics that turn long articles with lots of information into visual data that you can understand and digest quickly. See pages 170–171 and 230–231.

VERSUS OR COMPARISON INFOGRAPHICS

Here, a battle takes place between two or more things, drawn out so we can clearly see their similarities and differences. See pages 12–13 and 98–99.

GRAPHS

These are classic bar graphs showing the relationship between quantities that you might use in school, laid out on x and y axes, but we've spiced them up a bit for you. See pages 32–33 and 216–217.

BUBBLE CHARTS

These infographics display data in the form of bubbles or other objects, in which the biggest ones represent the biggest numbers. A comparison of size clearly conveys the differences among the data points. See pages 158–159 and 224–225.

TIME LINES

These are stories illustrated through chronological dates that will take you on a journey from start to finish. See pages 20–21.

Meet the **EXPERTS!**

IN *BY THE NUMBERS 2.0*, YOU'LL ALSO LEARN EVERYTHING YOU WANTED TO KNOW ABOUT AWESOME PEOPLE WORKING IN THE FIELD OF MATH AND NUMBERS. YOU'LL GET ADVICE ON MATH, SCIENCE, AND HOW TO BECOME A NUMBERS WHIZ. PLUS, LEARN EXACTLY WHAT MAKES THEIR JOBS SO COOL.

The bees you see buzzing around your garden are an important part of our life on Earth. By carrying pollen between flowers, they help us grow many of the foods we eat every day. Read on to learn more about these hardworking insects.

2 PAIRS OF WINGS

A bee's wings beat about 200 times per second, creating that famous "buzz" sound.

5 EYES

A bee has 2 large compound eyes and 3 small simple eyes on the top of its head.

6 LEGS

Hind legs have 2 areas called pollen baskets to help carry food back to the hive.

2 ANTENNAE

Each antenna has thousands of scent receptors to help bees smell.

ONE BEE FLIES UP TO

20

MILES AN HOUR
(32 km/h).

ONE BEE CAN FLY UP TO

6

MILES WITHOUT A BREAK
(10 km).

ONE HIVE CAN MAKE UP TO

100

POUNDS OF HONEY PER YEAR
(45 kg).

ONE BEE VISITS UP TO

100

FLOWERS PER TRIP.

A QUEEN BEE
USUALLY LIVES

2-3

YEARS IN THE WILD.

ONE HIVE OF BEES
CAN TRAVEL MORE THAN

50,000

MILES (80,467 km) TO MAKE
1 POUND (0.5 kg) OF HONEY.

THAT'S THE SAME AS

2

TRIPS AROUND EARTH
AT THE EQUATOR!

MEATLESS MIND-SET

Could you give up eating meat for a day? How about your whole life? Vegetarians are people who choose not to eat meat. Some people go a step further and avoid animal products, such as milk and eggs, altogether. How common is this dietary decision? Travel around the world and see how many people are going vegetarian.

CANADA

4%

USA

5%

2%
OF AMERICANS ARE VEGANS WHO EAT NO ANIMAL PRODUCTS.

36%
OF AMERICANS EAT AT LEAST 1 MEATLESS MEAL PER WEEK.

TOFU, A VEGETARIAN PROTEIN SOURCE MADE FROM SOYBEANS, WAS FIRST MADE IN CHINA MORE THAN **2,000 YEARS AGO.**

BRAZIL

8%

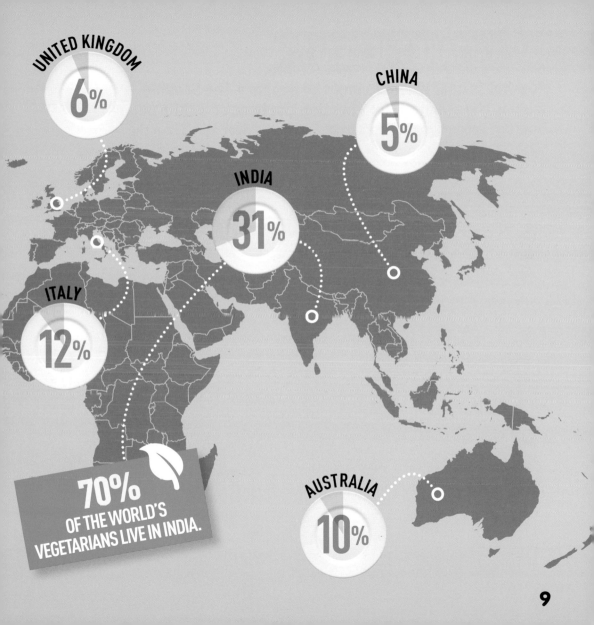

UNITED KINGDOM
6%

CHINA
5%

INDIA
31%

ITALY
12%

70%
OF THE WORLD'S
VEGETARIANS LIVE IN INDIA.

AUSTRALIA
10%

CAN YOU **TAKE THE HEAT?**

How hot is hot? When it comes to peppers, the Scoville scale is the standard for charting the heat of a chile pepper. From bell peppers to the flaming hot Carolina Reaper, here's how the most common peppers compare.

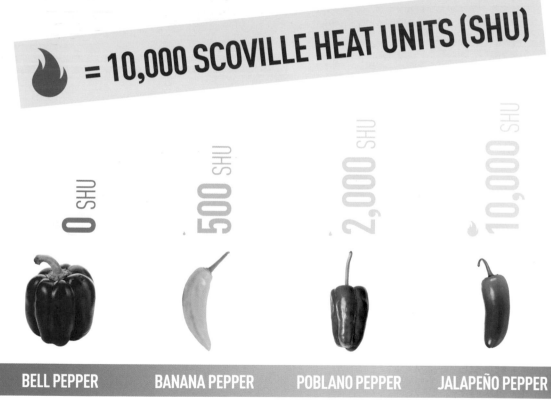

= 10,000 SCOVILLE HEAT UNITS (SHU)

0 SHU

500 SHU

2,000 SHU

10,000 SHU

BELL PEPPER **BANANA PEPPER** **POBLANO PEPPER** **JALAPEÑO PEPPER**

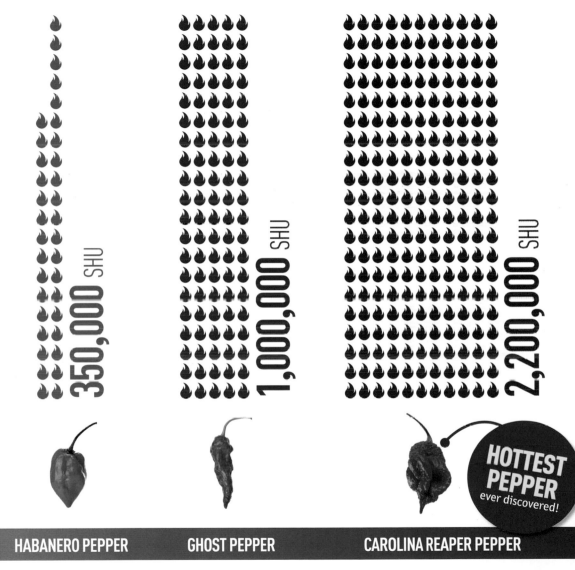

350,000 SHU

1,000,000 SHU

2,200,000 SHU

HOTTEST PEPPER ever discovered!

HABANERO PEPPER

GHOST PEPPER

CAROLINA REAPER PEPPER

Have you ever wondered why you see the **flash of lightning** before you hear the rumble of thunder? Here's why!

Sound travels at the superfast speed of

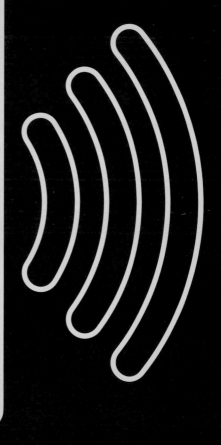

770

MILES AN HOUR

(1,239 km/h).

But that's nothing compared to light, which travels at

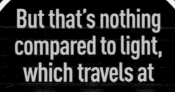

670,616,629
MILES AN HOUR
(1,079,252,848 km/h).

THAT'S 871,000 TIMES FASTER THAN SOUND!

PYRAMID PUZZLER

The Pyramids at Giza are some of the most mysterious structures in the world. How did the ancient Egyptians build such a massive structure without modern tools? Nobody knows for sure, but here are a few theories.

An estimated

40,000

Egyptians worked to construct the pyramids.

The largest stone blocks weighed up to

9 TONS

(8.2 t) each!

RAMPS

ARCHAEOLOGICAL EVIDENCE SHOWS THAT THE EGYPTIANS MIGHT HAVE USED ZIGZAGGING RAMPS, LEVERS, SLEDS, AND OTHER SIMPLE MACHINES TO MOVE THE MASSIVE STONES.

ROLLING

WHILE THE ANCIENT EGYPTIANS HADN'T DISCOVERED PULLEYS, THEY MAY HAVE USED WOODEN RODS TO HELP ROLL THE STONES ACROSS THE SAND.

CONCRETE

ANCIENT EGYPTIANS MIGHT HAVE MIXED LIMESTONE WITH WATER TO FORM A CONCRETE-LIKE CLAY. THEN, THEY CARRIED THE CLAY TO THE CONSTRUCTION SITE AND MOLDED IT INTO BLOCKS.

WET SAND

STONES GLIDE MORE EASILY OVER WET SAND, SO THE EGYPTIANS MAY HAVE USED WATER FROM THE NILE RIVER TO MOISTEN THE SAND BEFORE PUSHING OR PULLING A SLED TO THE BUILDING SITE.

The ancient Egyptians added

24 BLOCKS

to the pyramids every hour. That's 1 block every 2.5 minutes!

What's the most popular word in the English language? "The" answer might surprise you! These 25 words make up 1/3 of all printed material in English.

1.the

2.of 3.and

4.a 5.to 6.in

7. is   8. you   9. that

10. it   11. he   12. was

13. for   14. on   15. are

16. as   17. with   18. his

19. they   20. I   21. at   22. be

23. this   24. have   25. from

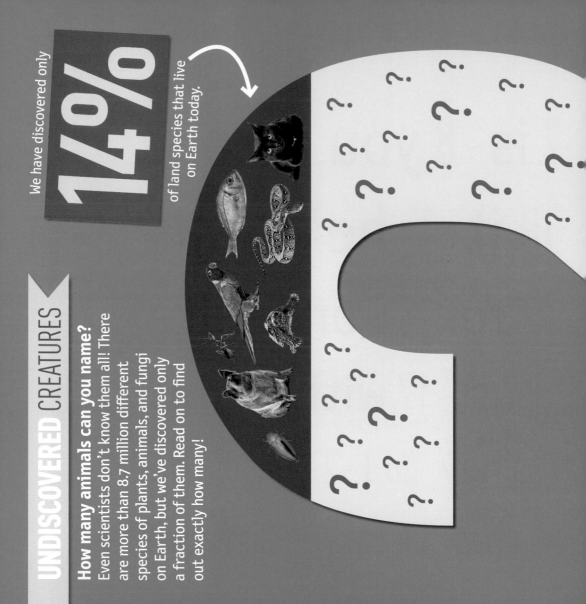

UNDISCOVERED CREATURES

How many animals can you name?
Even scientists don't know them all! There are more than 8.7 million different species of plants, animals, and fungi on Earth, but we've discovered only a fraction of them. Read on to find out exactly how many!

We have discovered only

14%

of land species that live on Earth today.

Scientists discover up to **18,000** new species each year!

That means **86%** of Earth's land species have yet to be discovered!

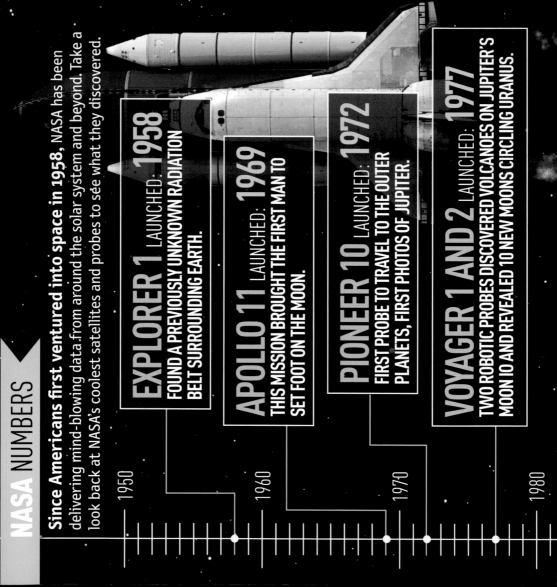

NASA NUMBERS

Since Americans first ventured into space in 1958, NASA has been delivering mind-blowing data from around the solar system and beyond. Take a look back at NASA's coolest satellites and probes to see what they discovered.

EXPLORER 1 LAUNCHED: **1958**
FOUND A PREVIOUSLY UNKNOWN RADIATION BELT SURROUNDING EARTH.

APOLLO 11 LAUNCHED: **1969**
THIS MISSION BROUGHT THE FIRST MAN TO SET FOOT ON THE MOON.

PIONEER 10 LAUNCHED: **1972**
FIRST PROBE TO TRAVEL TO THE OUTER PLANETS, FIRST PHOTOS OF JUPITER.

VOYAGER 1 AND 2 LAUNCHED: **1977**
TWO ROBOTIC PROBES DISCOVERED VOLCANOES ON JUPITER'S MOON IO AND REVEALED 10 NEW MOONS CIRCLING URANUS.

1950

1960

1970

1980

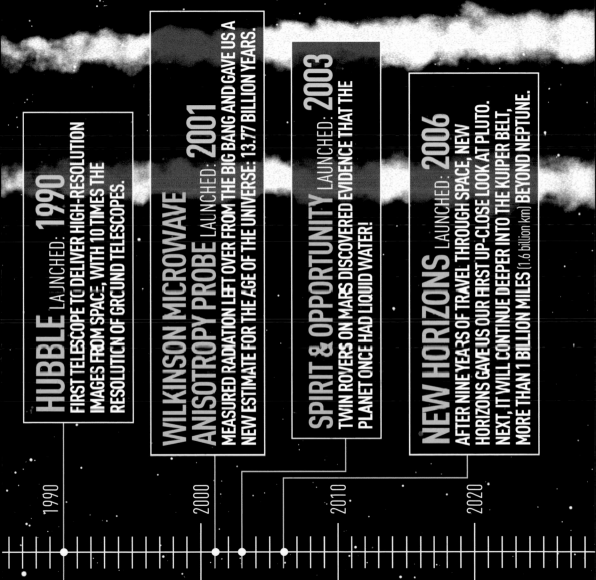

HUBBLE LAUNCHED: 1990
FIRST TELESCOPE TO DELIVER HIGH-RESOLUTION IMAGES FROM SPACE, WITH 10 TIMES THE RESOLUTION OF GROUND TELESCOPES.

WILKINSON MICROWAVE ANISOTROPY PROBE LAUNCHED: 2001
MEASURED RADIATION LEFT OVER FROM THE BIG BANG AND GAVE US A NEW ESTIMATE FOR THE AGE OF THE UNIVERSE: 13.77 BILLION YEARS.

SPIRIT & OPPORTUNITY LAUNCHED: 2003
TWIN ROVERS ON MARS DISCOVERED EVIDENCE THAT THE PLANET ONCE HAD LIQUID WATER!

NEW HORIZONS LAUNCHED: 2006
AFTER NINE YEARS OF TRAVEL THROUGH SPACE, NEW HORIZONS GAVE US OUR FIRST UP-CLOSE LOOK AT PLUTO. NEXT, IT WILL CONTINUE DEEPER INTO THE KUIPER BELT, MORE THAN 1 BILLION MILES (1.6 billion km) BEYOND NEPTUNE.

1990
2000
2010
2020

LAND OF **LEGOS**

Who loves LEGOs? Everyone!
With more than 600 billion LEGO pieces in production, LEGO is a worldwide phenomenon. See how these popular plastic bricks stack up.

1949 YEAR LEGOS WERE INVENTED

THAT'S **1,268** PIECES EVERY SECOND!

600 BILLION TOTAL NUMBER OF LEGO PIECES MADE

40 BILLION NUMBER OF LEGO BRICKS MADE EACH YEAR

40 BILLION NUMBER OF LEGO BRICKS YOU'D NEED TO STACK TO REACH THE MOON

318 MILLION NUMBER OF TINY RUBBER TIRES MADE AT THE LEGO FACTORY EACH YEAR

THAT MAKES LEGO THE WORLD'S LARGEST RUBBER TIRE MANUFACTURER!

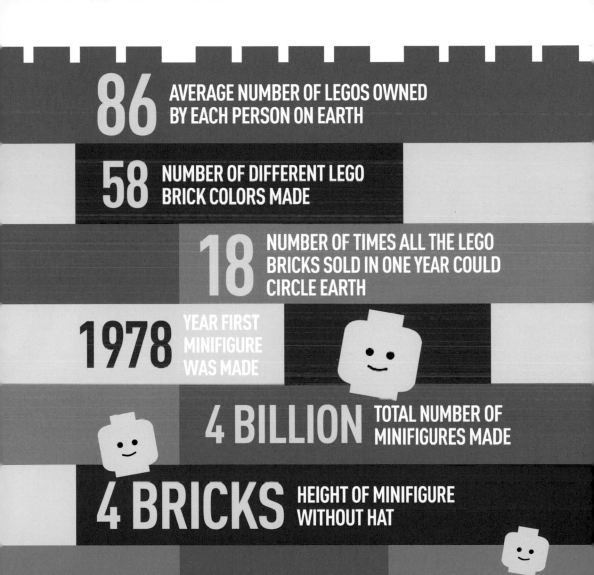

86 AVERAGE NUMBER OF LEGOS OWNED BY EACH PERSON ON EARTH

58 NUMBER OF DIFFERENT LEGO BRICK COLORS MADE

18 NUMBER OF TIMES ALL THE LEGO BRICKS SOLD IN ONE YEAR COULD CIRCLE EARTH

1978 YEAR FIRST MINIFIGURE WAS MADE

4 BILLION TOTAL NUMBER OF MINIFIGURES MADE

4 BRICKS HEIGHT OF MINIFIGURE WITHOUT HAT

WHAT'S BUGGING YOU?

Buzzing, stinging, crawling, and biting—some pests can really be annoying. Here's a look at some of the most irritating pests in the great outdoors.

1 OUT OF 5

Number of people who are mosquito magnets, attracting more bites than the average person

MOSQUITO

.0001 ounce (3 mg)

Amount of blood a mosquito drinks per bite

50

Number of eggs a female flea can produce per day. That's more than 2,000 eggs over its two-to-three-month life span.

FLEA

1998

Year first brown marmorated stink bug was spotted in Pennsylvania. The bugs are native to Asia and hitched a ride on cargo ships.

STINK BUG

$37 MILLION

Total damage to mid-Atlantic orchards in 2010 thanks to hungry stink bugs, which are known to eat 300 different plants

A single female tick can grow up to

2 TIMES

its size after feeding on blood for several days.

885

Number of different tick species all over the world

TICK

NOW THAT'S A **BIG PIE!**

You'd better be hungry if you want to eat a slice of this giant pizza! Five chefs in Italy teamed up to make the largest round pizza on Earth. Here's the supersized recipe.

1,488 POUNDS
(675 kg) OF **MARGARINE**

10,000 POUNDS
(4,536 kg) OF **TOMATO SAUCE**

19,800
POUNDS (8,981 kg)
OF **FLOUR**

131 FEET (40 m)
IN DIAMETER

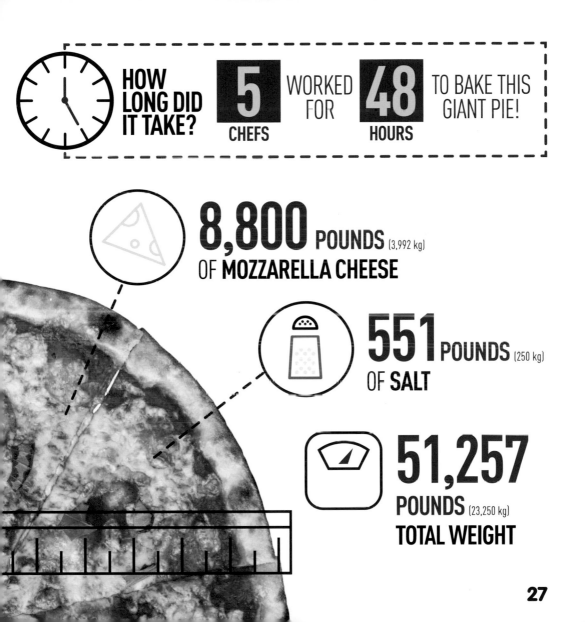

HOW LONG DID IT TAKE? **5** CHEFS WORKED FOR **48** HOURS TO BAKE THIS GIANT PIE!

8,800 POUNDS (3,992 kg) OF **MOZZARELLA CHEESE**

551 POUNDS (250 kg) OF **SALT**

51,257 POUNDS (23,250 kg) **TOTAL WEIGHT**

27

BOVINE BATHROOM BREAK

Cows can eat up to
100 POUNDS
(45 kg) of feed every day.

Cows can drink up to
35 GALLONS
(133 l) of water every day.

COWS POOP 16 TIMES EVERY DAY,

TOTALING UP TO **65 POUNDS** (30 kg) OF MANURE.
THAT'S ABOUT THE WEIGHT OF A **10-YEAR-OLD!**

BASKETBALL **NUMBERS**

He shoots, he scores! Brush up on your basketball knowledge with these fast facts.

1891:
Basketball is invented by Dr. James Naismith as a new sport that kids could play during the cold winter months. His original game had 13 rules. He split his 18 students into 2 teams of 9 players each. The score of the first game ever played was 1 to 0.

1906:
After initially playing with peach baskets, new metal hoops, nets, and backboards are introduced. Today, the basket's metal rim has a diameter of 18 inches (46 cm) and is 10 feet (3 m) above the court floor.

1946:
The second official basketball league is formed. Originally called the Basketball Association of America, the group changed its name to the National Basketball Association, or NBA, just 3 years later in 1949.

1898:
First official basketball league is formed. It had 6 teams. The very first champions were the Trenton Nationals. The league was closed down 6 years later in 1904.

1962:

Wilt Chamberlain sets a new NBA record, scoring 100 points in a single game.

1996:

Michael Jordan stars in the animated basketball movie *Space Jam*. It's the most successful basketball movie of all time, making $230 million when it is released.

1987:

Manute Bol and Muggsy Bogues are both drafted to the Bullets, putting the world's tallest and shortest basketball players on the same team. Manute measures 7 feet 7 inches (2.31 m) tall, while Muggsy is 5 feet 3 inches (1.6 m) tall.

2002:

At 17 years old, LeBron James is featured on the cover of *Sports Illustrated*. He was only in the 11th grade!

1989:

Kareem Abdul-Jabbar retires from the NBA with a record-breaking 38,387 points scored over 1,560 games.

2016:

Kobe Bryant will make $25 million in what could be his final season in the NBA.

SEAHORSE **0.001 MPH** (0.002 km/h)

GOLDFISH **0.85 MPH** (1.4 km/h)

MICHAEL PHELPS **4.5 MPH** (7.1 km/h)

SHORTFIN MAKO SHARK **31 MPH** (50 km/h)

FOUR-WINGED FLYING FISH **35 MPH** (56 km/h)

MARLIN **50 MPH*** (80 km/h)

* Burst or leaping speed

32

PHELPS SWAM THE
100-METER BUTTERFLY IN
50.58 SECONDS
DURING THE 2008 SUMMER
OLYMPICS, SETTING
A NEW RECORD.

**Michael Phelps is one of the
fastest swimmers in the world.**
He's won 18 Olympic gold medals, but how
does he compare to these sea creatures?
Here's how Phelps's speed stacks up.

A sailfish can measure
up to
11 FEET
(3.4 m) long. The sailfish uses its
razor-sharp bill to stun prey
and folds its tall fin back to
swim at record-breaking
speeds.

SAILFISH **68 MPH*** (109 km/h)

Video-sharing site YouTube is an Internet sensation, racking up more than one billion users since it was founded in 2005. Nearly 1 out of every 7 people on Earth use YouTube! Tune in to learn more about this virtual video vault.

THE AVERAGE MOBILE USER WATCHES VIDEOS FOR

40 MINUTES

AT A TIME!

YOUTUBE IS THE **3rd** MOST POPULAR WEBSITE ON THE INTERNET, BEHIND GOOGLE AND FACEBOOK.

EVERY DAY, YOUTUBE USERS GENERATE

4 BILLION VIEWS.

400 HOURS OF VIDEO ARE UPLOADED TO YOUTUBE EVERY MINUTE.

THAT'S 1,000 DAYS OF VIDEO UPLOADED EVERY HOUR!

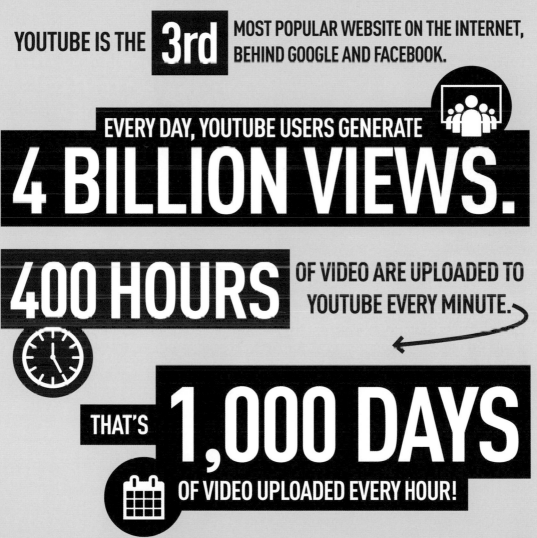

AN INTERVIEW WITH DATA SCIENTIST CARLOS F. MEDINA RAMIREZ

CARLOS IS **SAVING THE WORLD** WITH THE POWER OF **NUMBERS!** BY USING DATA TO FIGURE OUT HOW TO GET **CLEAN WATER** TO THE PEOPLE WHO NEED IT MOST, CARLOS HAS HELPED MORE THAN

5,600,000

PEOPLE AROUND THE WORLD. HERE'S HOW!

Q: WHAT DO YOU DO?

A: charity: water provides clean and safe drinking water to villages in developing countries that do not have access to it. My work helps the people in our organization make the best decisions possible, so that we can reach people in a better way. I look at all the information we have regarding water projects and our supporters, and try to find hidden patterns there.

Q: WHAT KINDS OF PROBLEMS HAVE YOU SOLVED WITH NUMBERS?

A: Sometimes our water projects are in places hard to get to, and we aren't sure if they are working well. So, I built a model that tells us, based on just six questions, if the water project is likely to be working well or not. This will allow us to keep the water flowing in those villages that might need it the most.

Q: WHEN DID YOU FIRST BECOME INTERESTED IN MATH?

A: It was during a class called "Mathematics in the Sciences and the Arts." My teacher taught me how to look at nature, music, and art through a mathematical lens so I could learn to appreciate them in a deeper way.

Q: WHAT'S YOUR FAVORITE THING ABOUT NUMBERS?

A: Numbers tell us stories that are not easy to see for the untrained eye, but if you learn how to see them, it enriches the whole world around you.

FAST-FOOD FACTS

Want fries with that? Every month, kids between the ages of 6 and 14 eat fast food 157,000,000 times. Before you dig in, read on to find out just how many calories you're eating during an average fast-food feast.

MENU

1/4-POUND CHEESEBURGER
520 Calories

MEDIUM FRENCH FRIES
380

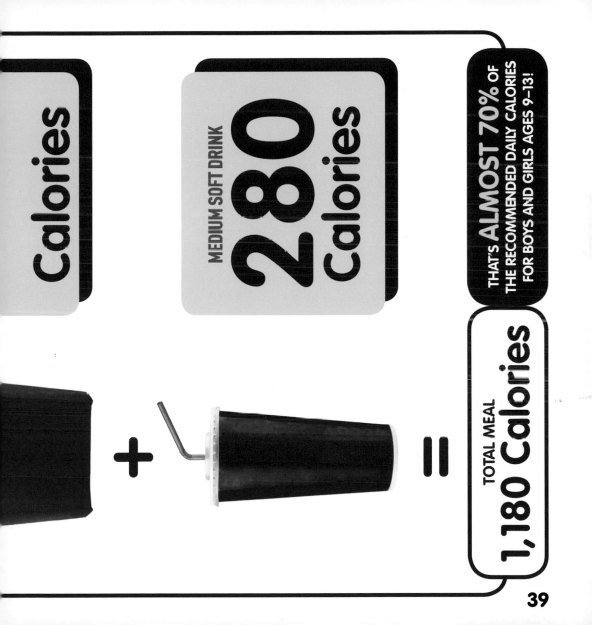

Calories

MEDIUM SOFT DRINK

280 Calories

THAT'S **ALMOST 70%** OF THE RECOMMENDED DAILY CALORIES FOR BOYS AND GIRLS AGES 9–13!

+ =

TOTAL MEAL
1,180 Calories

What's the boniest part of your body?

Raise your hands and feet! More than half the bones in your entire body are in your extremities. Want to find out exactly how many? Let's start counting!

14
PHALANGES
finger bones

5
METACARPALS
palm bones

8
CARPALS
wrist bones

**27
BONES
in each hand**

14
PHALANGES
toe bones

5
METATARSALS
sole bones

26
BONES
in each foot

7
TARSALS
ankle bones

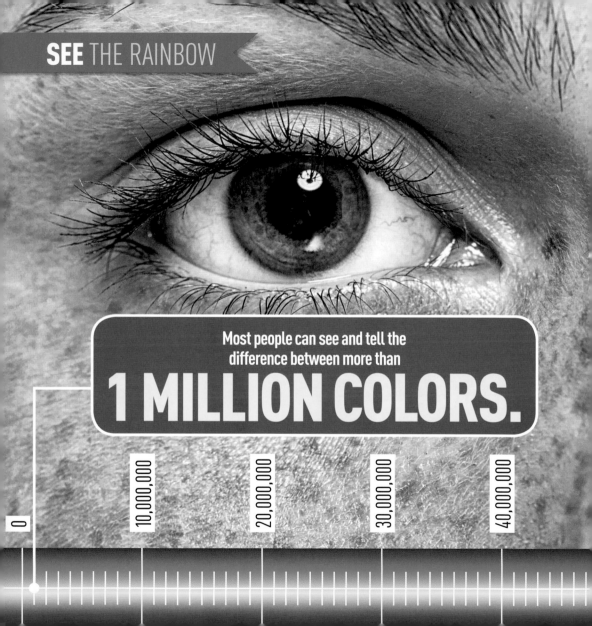

SEE THE RAINBOW

Most people can see and tell the difference between more than

1 MILLION COLORS.

0

10,000,000

20,000,000

30,000,000

40,000,000

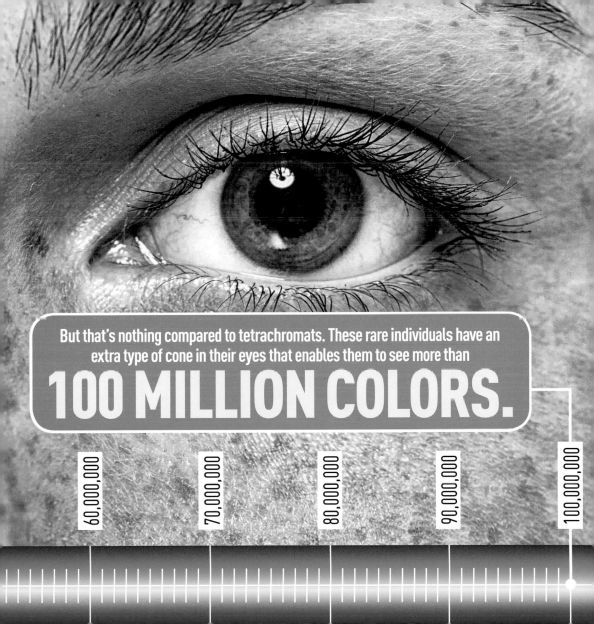

But that's nothing compared to tetrachromats. These rare individuals have an extra type of cone in their eyes that enables them to see more than

100 MILLION COLORS.

60,000,000

70,000,000

80,000,000

90,000,000

100,000,000

PECKING **THE DAY AWAY**

The next time you're in the woods, listen closely, and you might hear the tapping sound of a woodpecker using its strong bill and sticky tongue to hunt for lunch. Here are some fast facts about these feathered friends.

A WOODPECKER CAN **PECK** UP TO **20** TIMES PER SECOND

AT A **SPEED** OF **15** MILES AN HOUR. (24 km/h)

THAT'S **8,000–12,000** PECKS PER DAY.

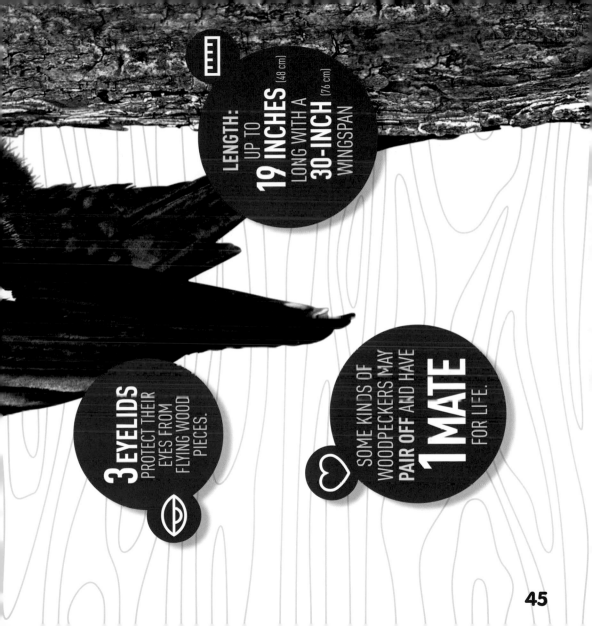

LENGTH: UP TO **19 INCHES** (48 cm) LONG WITH A **30-INCH** (76 cm) WINGSPAN

3 EYELIDS PROTECT THEIR EYES FROM FLYING WOOD PIECES.

SOME KINDS OF WOODPECKERS MAY **PAIR OFF** AND HAVE **1 MATE** FOR LIFE.

FLUSHER FIGURES

Time for a bathroom break! But before you go, here are some disgusting details about the porcelain throne.

THE AVERAGE PERSON SPENDS
1 HOUR AND 42 MINUTES
SITTING ON THE TOILET EACH WEEK.

THAT'S ALMOST **92 DAYS** OF YOUR LIFE!

THE AVERAGE PERSON USES THE TOILET
2,500 TIMES A YEAR.

TYPES OF BACTERIA FOUND IN AVERAGE BATHROOM:
19

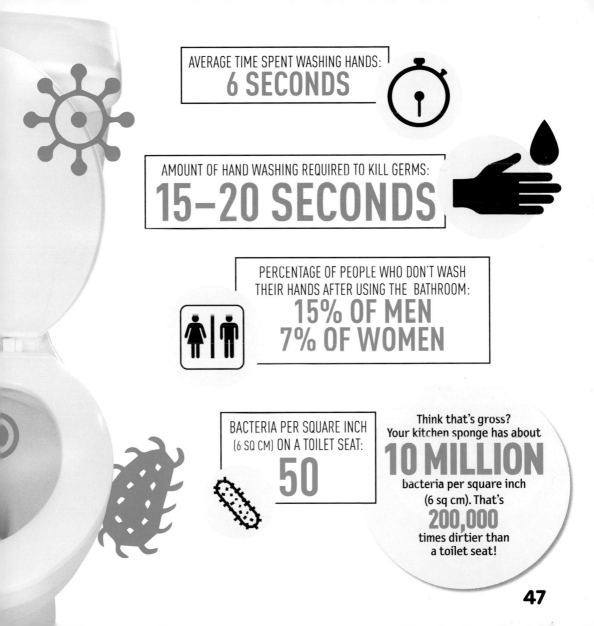

AVERAGE TIME SPENT WASHING HANDS:
6 SECONDS

AMOUNT OF HAND WASHING REQUIRED TO KILL GERMS:
15–20 SECONDS

PERCENTAGE OF PEOPLE WHO DON'T WASH THEIR HANDS AFTER USING THE BATHROOM:
15% OF MEN
7% OF WOMEN

BACTERIA PER SQUARE INCH (6 SQ CM) ON A TOILET SEAT:
50

Think that's gross? Your kitchen sponge has about **10 MILLION** bacteria per square inch (6 sq cm). That's **200,000** times dirtier than a toilet seat!

It's July 4. After a day of celebration, the sun has set and all eyes are on the sky. Then you hear it. Boom! Crack! All of a sudden, a rainbow of dazzling colors explodes across the sky. Fireworks are science in action! Here's the chemical reaction at work in every sparkly shot.

FIREWORKS SHOT
DURING THE FOURTH OF JULY:
225 MILLION
POUNDS
(102 million kg)

SPEED OF
FIREWORK ROCKET:
150 MILES
AN HOUR
(241 km/h)

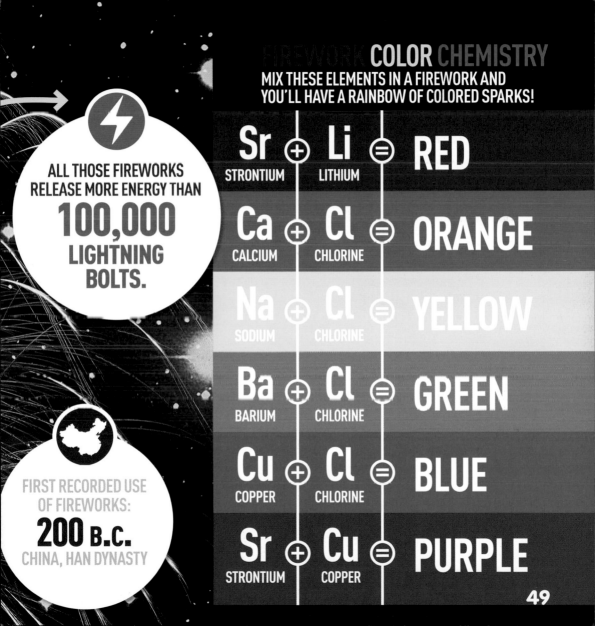

FIREWORK COLOR CHEMISTRY

MIX THESE ELEMENTS IN A FIREWORK AND YOU'LL HAVE A RAINBOW OF COLORED SPARKS!

Sr + **Li** = **RED**
STRONTIUM LITHIUM

Ca + **Cl** = **ORANGE**
CALCIUM CHLORINE

Na + **Cl** = **YELLOW**
SODIUM CHLORINE

Ba + **Cl** = **GREEN**
BARIUM CHLORINE

Cu + **Cl** = **BLUE**
COPPER CHLORINE

Sr + **Cu** = **PURPLE**
STRONTIUM COPPER

ALL THOSE FIREWORKS RELEASE MORE ENERGY THAN **100,000** LIGHTNING BOLTS.

FIRST RECORDED USE OF FIREWORKS: **200 B.C.** CHINA, HAN DYNASTY

49

The world's fastest car is more than

38 TIMES

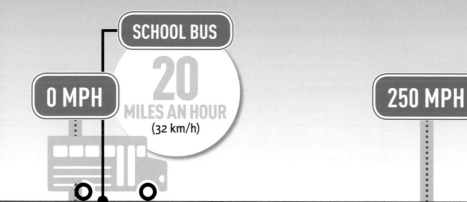

SCHOOL BUS

0 MPH

20 MILES AN HOUR (32 km/h)

250 MPH

HOW'D THE CAR GO THAT FAST? The car is powered

FASTER

than a bus driving in a school zone!

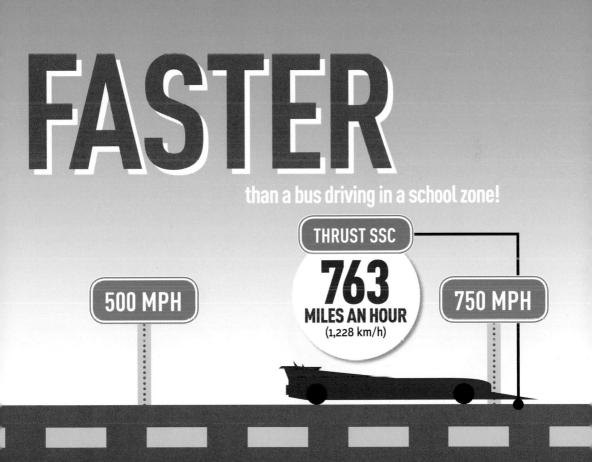

THRUST SSC

763
MILES AN HOUR
(1,228 km/h)

500 MPH

750 MPH

by **2 JET ENGINES** that generate **50,000 POUNDS** (22,680 kg) of thrust!

AMUSEMENT PARK ANTICS

Come one, come all! There's plenty of fun to be had at the theme park, from exciting rides to delicious snacks. More than 376 million people enjoy visiting amusement parks every year. Here's your ticket to the country's most popular parks.

714
Number of roller coasters in the United States as of 2015.

550
FEET (168 m)
Height of the High Roller in Las Vegas, the largest Ferris wheel in the world

20 MILLION
Number of LEGO bricks used at LEGOLAND California to create Miniland USA, a collection of miniature 1:20 scale LEGO versions of U.S. landmarks such as the Empire State Building and the White House

400+
Number of amusement parks in the United States

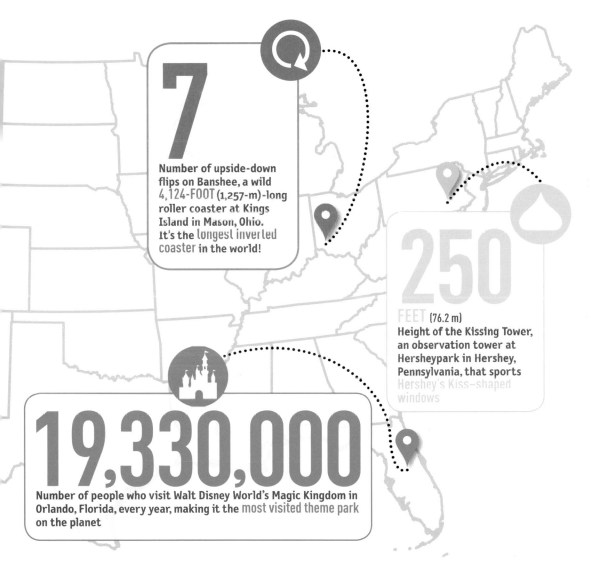

7

Number of upside-down flips on Banshee, a wild 4,124-FOOT (1,257-m)-long roller coaster at Kings Island in Mason, Ohio. It's the longest inverted coaster in the world!

250

FEET (76.2 m)
Height of the Kissing Tower, an observation tower at Hersheypark in Hershey, Pennsylvania, that sports Hershey's Kiss–shaped windows

19,330,000

Number of people who visit Walt Disney World's Magic Kingdom in Orlando, Florida, every year, making it the most visited theme park on the planet

PASS THE GAS

Passing gas, breaking wind, cutting the cheese.
Doctors call it "flatulence." Whatever you call it, we all do it!
Plug your nose and prepare to learn more about these
stinky gaseous emissions.

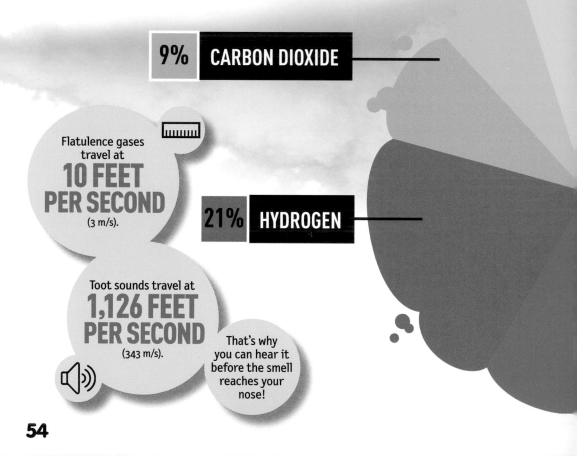

9% CARBON DIOXIDE

Flatulence gases travel at
10 FEET PER SECOND
(3 m/s).

21% HYDROGEN

Toot sounds travel at
1,126 FEET PER SECOND
(343 m/s).

That's why you can hear it before the smell reaches your nose!

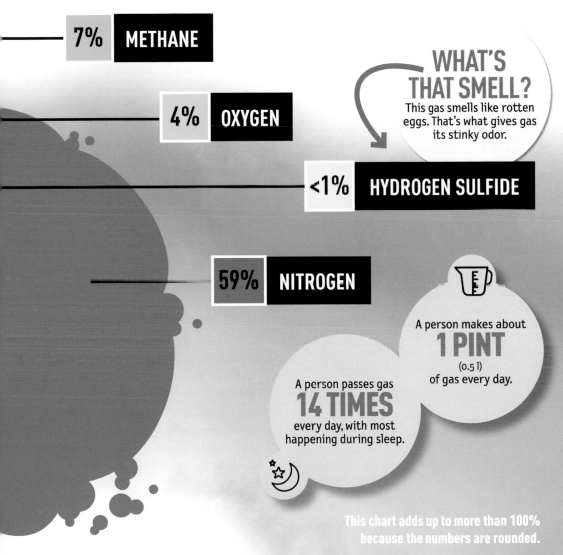

7% METHANE

4% OXYGEN

WHAT'S THAT SMELL?
This gas smells like rotten eggs. That's what gives gas its stinky odor.

<1% HYDROGEN SULFIDE

59% NITROGEN

A person makes about
1 PINT
(0.5 l)
of gas every day.

A person passes gas
14 TIMES
every day, with most happening during sleep.

This chart adds up to more than 100% because the numbers are rounded.

THE SCOOP ON ICE CREAM

When the weather's hot, a frozen treat hits the spot.
This dairy delight is a summer must-have, and we're eating it up—millions of gallons at a time! Read on for some delectable dairy facts.

AMERICANS ARE THE

#1

CONSUMERS OF ICE CREAM WORLDWIDE.

MOST SCOOPS BALANCED ON 1 CONE:

100

25%

OF ALL SCOOPS SOLD ARE VANILLA.

10% OF MILK PRODUCED BY U.S. DAIRY FARMERS IS USED TO MAKE ICE CREAM.

YEAR ICE CREAM CONE INVENTED:

1904

President George Washington spent **$200** on ice cream during the hot summer of **1790.**

That would be **$5,340** today!

THE AVERAGE AMERICAN EATS ALMOST **22 POUNDS** (10 KG) OF ICE CREAM PER YEAR.

TELEVISION TRIVIA

Do you have a TV in your house? With more than 243 million televisions in homes across the United States, there's a 99 percent chance that you have one—and watch it every day. But is it possible to have too much of a good thing? Tune in to these shocking TV stats.

KIDS SPEND

44 HOURS

PER WEEK IN FRONT OF TV, COMPUTER, AND GAME SCREENS.

The only activity kids do more often?

SLEEP!

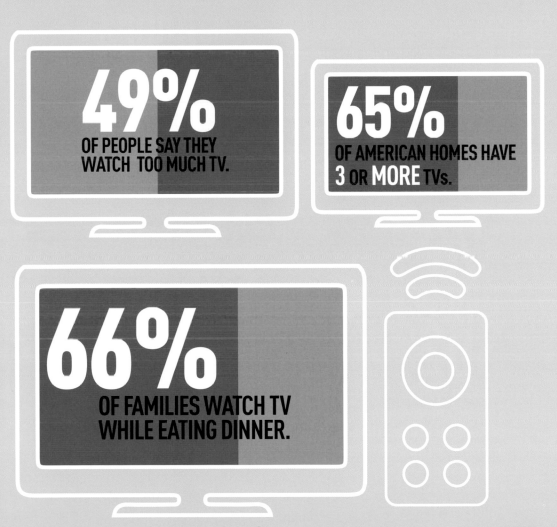

49% OF PEOPLE SAY THEY WATCH TOO MUCH TV.

65% OF AMERICAN HOMES HAVE 3 OR MORE TVs.

66% OF FAMILIES WATCH TV WHILE EATING DINNER.

SPIDERWEB STATS

A single spider can eat up to 2,000 insects every year. How do spiders catch all of those tasty treats? Using silk from special glands called spinnerets, spiders weave sticky webs to trap their delicious prey. But this silk can do much more than simply catch dinner. Stick around and learn more about the incredible spiderweb.

.00004-.00016
INCH (.001-.004 mm)
Thickness of silk a spider uses to build webs

-76°F THROUGH 302°F
(-60°C to 150°C)
The extreme range of temperatures that a spider's silk can withstand

82
FEET (25 m)
Diameter of webs woven by Darwin's bark spider—the largest spiderwebs in the world!

2-8

Pairs of spinnerets, the glands a spider uses to make silk

5

Number of times stronger spider's silk is, compared to steel of the same diameter

Age of oldest spiderweb ever found embedded in amber:

140 MILLION

YEARS OLD

MYSTERIOUS MARIANA TRENCH

Although more than 70 percent of the planet is covered by oceans, we've only just begun to uncover the mysteries of the sea. Dive into the deepest recorded part of the ocean for some mind-blowing facts.

If you put Mount Everest at the bottom of the Mariana Trench, the peak would still be **6,792 FEET** (2,070 m) below sea level.

HEIGHT OF MOUNT EVEREST:

29,035 FEET
(8,850 m)

1,000 feet (305 m)

5,000 feet (1,524 m)

10,000 feet (3,048 m)

15,000 feet (4,572 m)

The Mariana Trench is **1,554 MILES** (2,501 km) long, more than **5 TIMES** longer than the Grand Canyon.

DEPTH OF MARIANA TRENCH: 35,827 FEET (10,920 m)

20,000 feet (6,096 m)

25,000 feet (7,620 m)

30,000 feet (9,144 m)

35,000 feet (10,668 m)

BIG SPENDERS

How much money is in your piggy bank? Here's how kids save (and spend!) their hard-earned cash.

13%
DEFINITELY A SAVER

24%
DEFINITELY A SPENDER

What do kids buy?

56% FOOD, CANDY, OR TREATS

56% GAMES

33%
**MORE OF
A SPENDER**

30%
**MORE OF
A SAVER**

46% CLOTHES

46% TOYS

39% ELECTRONICS

AMAZING ANIMAL EYES

Peer through the eyes of your favorite animals and find out what life looks like from their point of view.

Owls can see a moving mouse from

150 FEET

(46 m) **away.**

A dragonfly has
30,000 LENSES
in each eye, which help it see its prey.

A pigeon's brain can process visual information
3 TIMES FASTER
than a human's brain. That's why pigeons wait until the last minute to get out of your way—our movement appears slow to them.

Chameleons can look in
2 DIRECTIONS
at once.

Cats have about a **200°** field of vision.
A human's field of vision is only 180°.

DOLLAR DETAILS

Do you have a dollar bill in your piggy bank? You probably do, but do you know how it's made? Here's how the U.S. Department of Treasury prints money. Don't try this at home!

STEP 1 DOLLAR BILLS ARE PRINTED ON LARGE SHEETS IN MULTIPLES.
THERE ARE **32 BILLS** PER SHEET.

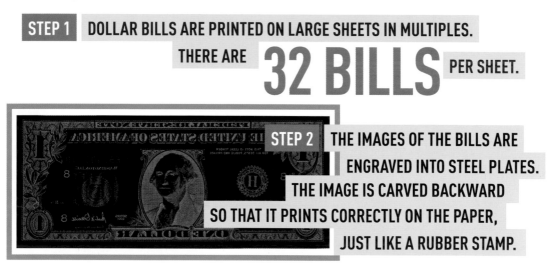

STEP 2 THE IMAGES OF THE BILLS ARE ENGRAVED INTO STEEL PLATES. THE IMAGE IS CARVED BACKWARD SO THAT IT PRINTS CORRECTLY ON THE PAPER, JUST LIKE A RUBBER STAMP.

STEP 3 THE PRINTING PLATE IS COATED WITH INK.
4 TONS (3.6 t) OF INK IS USED TO PRINT DOLLAR BILLS EVERY DAY.

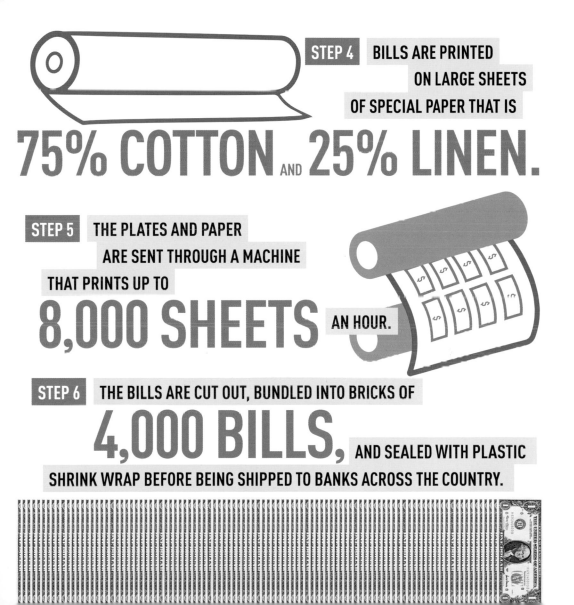

STEP 4 BILLS ARE PRINTED
ON LARGE SHEETS
OF SPECIAL PAPER THAT IS

75% COTTON AND 25% LINEN.

STEP 5 THE PLATES AND PAPER
ARE SENT THROUGH A MACHINE
THAT PRINTS UP TO

8,000 SHEETS AN HOUR.

STEP 6 THE BILLS ARE CUT OUT, BUNDLED INTO BRICKS OF

4,000 BILLS, AND SEALED WITH PLASTIC
SHRINK WRAP BEFORE BEING SHIPPED TO BANKS ACROSS THE COUNTRY.

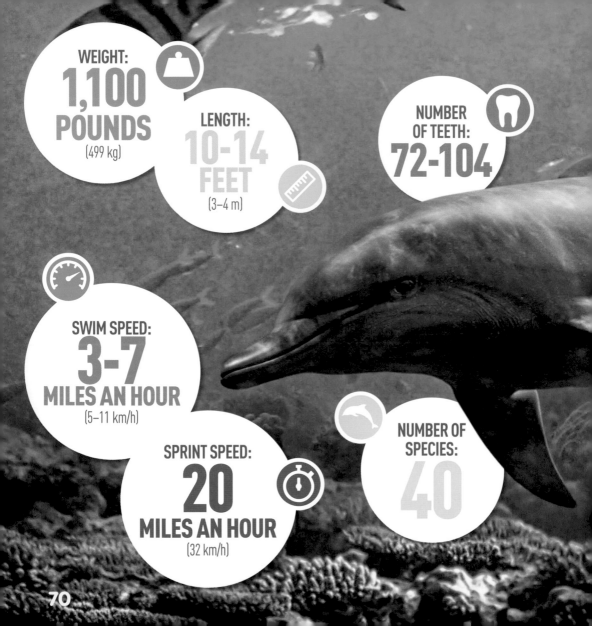

WEIGHT:
1,100 POUNDS
(499 kg)

LENGTH:
10-14 FEET
(3–4 m)

NUMBER OF TEETH:
72-104

SWIM SPEED:
3-7 MILES AN HOUR
(5–11 km/h)

SPRINT SPEED:
20 MILES AN HOUR
(32 km/h)

NUMBER OF SPECIES:
40

BODY TEMPERATURE:
98°F
(37°C)

DOLPHIN DATA

Swimming, dancing, and playing. Dolphins are fun to watch and fascinating, too. That's why they're the most studied marine mammals in the world! Dive into these cool dolphin facts.

JUMP HEIGHT:
UP TO 20 FEET
(6 m)

DISTANCE TRAVELED DAILY:
UP TO 40 MILES
(64 km)

DIVE DEPTH:
UP TO 150 FEET
(46 m)

TONS OF **TRASH**

A **FAMILY OF FOUR** GENERATES MORE THAN

6,000 POUNDS

[2,722 kg]

OF TRASH EACH YEAR.

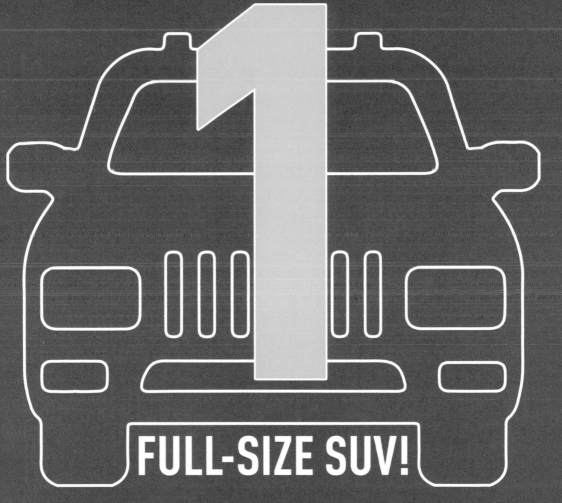

THAT'S AS HEAVY AS

1

FULL-SIZE SUV!

SURPRISING SPORTS STATS

Baseball, football, basketball, soccer— which sports do you play? Check out these facts about youth athletes.

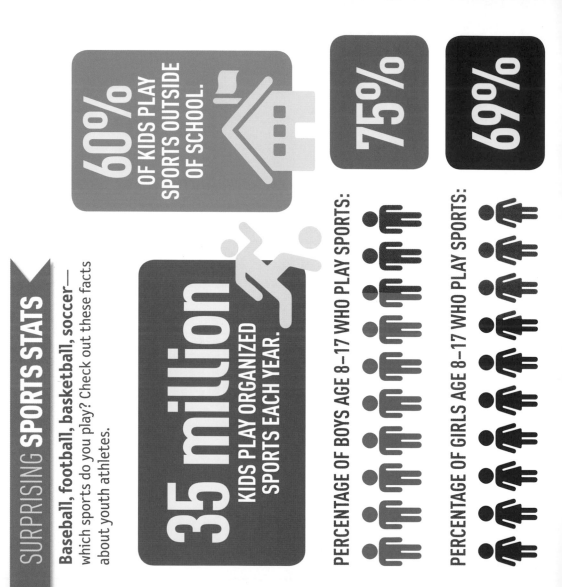

35 million KIDS PLAY ORGANIZED SPORTS EACH YEAR.

60% OF KIDS PLAY SPORTS OUTSIDE OF SCHOOL.

75%

69%

PERCENTAGE OF BOYS AGE 8–17 WHO PLAY SPORTS:

PERCENTAGE OF GIRLS AGE 8–17 WHO PLAY SPORTS:

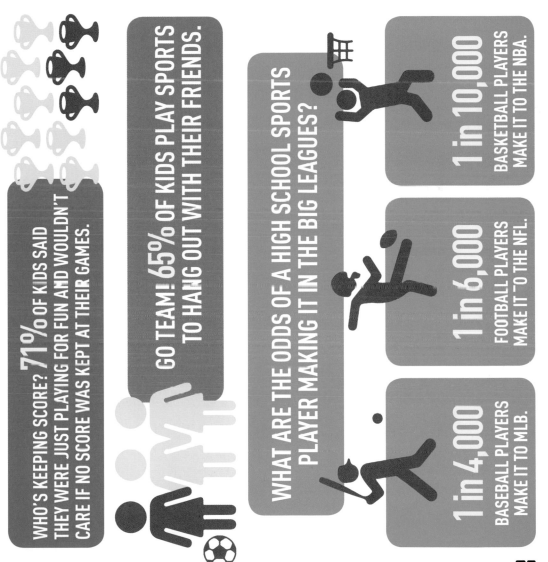

WHO'S KEEPING SCORE? 71% OF KIDS SAID THEY WERE JUST PLAYING FOR FUN AND WOULDN'T CARE IF NO SCORE WAS KEPT AT THEIR GAMES.

GO TEAM! 65% OF KIDS PLAY SPORTS TO HANG OUT WITH THEIR FRIENDS.

WHAT ARE THE ODDS OF A HIGH SCHOOL SPORTS PLAYER MAKING IT IN THE BIG LEAGUES?

1 in 10,000 BASKETBALL PLAYERS MAKE IT TO THE NBA.

1 in 6,000 FOOTBALL PLAYERS MAKE IT TO THE NFL.

1 in 4,000 BASEBALL PLAYERS MAKE IT TO MLB.

COUNTING COMETS

Shooting through space and circling around the sun, comets are balls of dirty ice that carry clues about the formation of our solar system around 4.6 billion years ago. As the comet passes near the sun, its ice heats up and releases dust and gases that make up its signature tail. Look up and see if you can spot one of these space snowballs!

NUMBER OF
COMETS DISCOVERED:
3,000+

YEAR NASA FIRST
SUCCESSFULLY LANDED A
PROBE ON A COMET:
2014

NUMBER OF UNDISCOVERED
COMETS THAT COULD BE
ORBITING THE SUN:
1 BILLION

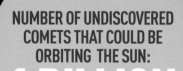

YEAR HALLEY'S
COMET WAS FIRST
SIGHTED:
240 B.C.

IT TAKES
200 YEARS OR LESS
FOR SHORT-PERIOD COMETS TO ORBIT THE SUN.

IT TAKES
200 YEARS OR MORE
FOR LONG-PERIOD COMETS TO ORBIT THE SUN.

Comet Hyakutake's tail measured more than
3 TIMES
the distance from Earth to the sun.

LENGTH OF LARGEST COMET TAIL EVER RECORDED:
360 MILLION MILES
(570 million km)

EVERY YEAR, ENOUGH BUBBLE WRAP IS MADE TO STRETCH AROUND THE WORLD

10 TIMES.

STRESSED OUT? BETTER GET POPPING! A 2012 SURVEY SHOWED THAT **1 MINUTE**

THAT'S NEARLY
250,000
MILES (402,336 km)
OF BUBBLE WRAP.

OF POPPING BUBBLE WRAP WAS AS RELAXING AS A **33-MINUTE** MASSAGE.

THE AVERAGE CHICKEN LAYS

300

EGGS

PER YEAR—ENOUGH TO FILL 25 EGG CARTONS!

YOU'VE GOT MAIL

Six days a week, the United States Postal Service delivers mail to more than 154 million addresses in every state, city, and town in the country. Here's a special delivery of postal service stats.

PIECES OF MAIL PROCESSED IN 2014:
155.4 billion

NUMBER OF POST OFFICES:
31,662

NUMBER OF POSTAL EMPLOYEES:
617,254

NUMBER OF MAIL TRUCKS:
211,264

NUMBER OF U.S. POSTAGE STAMPS PRINTED IN 2014:
19.4 billion

40%
OF ALL MAIL SENT ON EARTH IS HANDLED BY THE U.S. POSTAL SERVICE!

WHAT HAPPENS WHEN A NASA SPACECRAFT FLIES THROUGH JUPITER'S RADIATION BELT?

MEET >>

RACHEL BINX'S APP CAN TELL YOU THAT!

Q: WHAT DO YOU DO?

A: I make data visualization tools for NASA! I work on a web application that takes spacecraft data and turns it into charts and graphs.

Q: HAVE YOU ALWAYS LIKED MATH AND NUMBERS?

A: I've been interested in math from a young age. I loved thinking about numbers and logic puzzles. Math feels like discovering the secret rules that bind the universe together. Once you learn about a concept in math, you start to see it all around you!

RACHEL BINX, DATA VISUALIZATION ENGINEER AT NASA

Q: WHAT'S THE COOLEST DISCOVERY YOU'VE MADE?

A: I help spacecraft operators figure out what happened if something went wrong on their spacecraft. The longer that we can keep the spacecrafts operational, the more science data that they'll be able to collect, and the more that we'll know about our universe!

Q: WHAT'S YOUR ADVICE FOR ASPIRING SPACE SCIENTISTS?

A: Push yourself to try new things. I never would have dreamed that my interest in math would lead to working on space exploration!

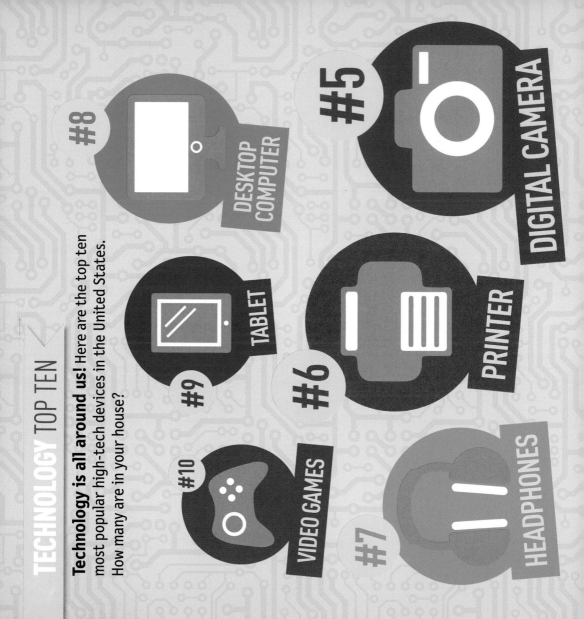

TECHNOLOGY TOP TEN

Technology is all around us! Here are the top ten most popular high-tech devices in the United States. How many are in your house?

#8 DESKTOP COMPUTER

#5 DIGITAL CAMERA

#9 TABLET

#6 PRINTER

#10 VIDEO GAMES

#7 HEADPHONES

#2

DVD PLAYER

#3

SMARTPHONE

#4

LAPTOP

TELEVISION

#1

WHERE DO AMERICANS **LIVE?**

There are about 321 million people living in the United States, but we don't all live in the same places. The different colors on this map represent areas of low and high population density. Can you tell which cities and states are packed with the most people?

LEAST POPULOUS CITY

MOST POPULOUS STATE
California
39,144,818

LEAST POPULOUS STATE
Wyoming
586,107

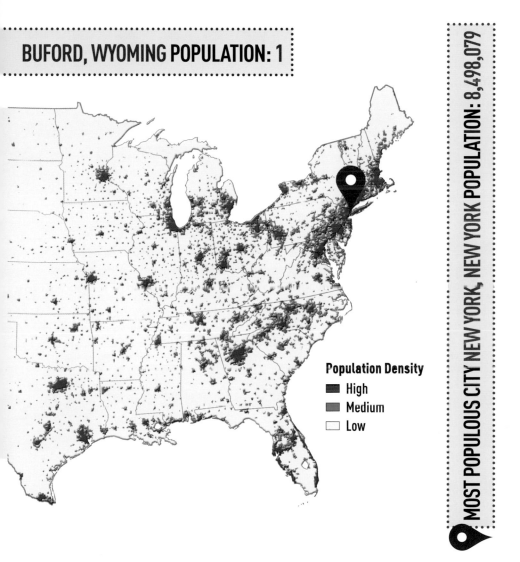

Population Density
- High
- Medium
- Low

A CRUNCHY LUNCH

Would you chomp on crickets for lunch?

All over the world, insects aren't just bugs. For two billion people living in Africa, Asia, and Latin America, edible insects are a normal item on the menu. Here's how much protein you'll get when you chow down on one serving (100 g) of these creepy crawlies.

HOUSEFLIES:

20

GRAMS OF PROTEIN

MILK:

8

GRAMS OF PROTEIN

MILK

ONE PINT (473mL)

CRICKETS:

25

GRAMS OF PROTEIN

GRASSHOPPERS:

48

GRAMS OF PROTEIN

I LIKE MY PEANUT BUTTER **EXTRA CRUNCHY!**

Chances are you're already eating bugs anyway! According to the FDA, peanut butter is allowed to contain up to

30 INSECT PARTS PER 100 GRAMS.

TERMITES:

28

GRAMS OF PROTEIN

SQUIRREL STATS

Peek outside your window, and chances are you'll spot one of these cute rodents. Squirrel away some of these facts for a rainy day!

FOOD EATEN WEEKLY:
1-1.5 POUNDS
(0.5–0.7 kg)
THAT'S MORE THAN THE SQUIRREL'S TOTAL BODY WEIGHT!

NUMBER OF TEETH:
20

A squirrel's
4 FRONT TEETH
never stop growing!

BIGGEST:
INDIAN GIANT SQUIRREL
3 FEET (1 m) LONG

SMALLEST:
AFRICAN PYGMY SQUIRREL
5 INCHES (13 cm) LONG

A SQUIRREL'S FUR CAN BE 1 OF 6 DIFFERENT COLORS:

RED **BROWN** **BLACK** **CREAM** **GRAY** **WHITE**

285

DIFFERENT SPECIES OF SQUIRREL

VERTICAL JUMP:

4-5 FEET

(1.2–1.5 m)

MOST COMMON SPECIES:
TREE SQUIRREL

COUNTING AT THE CAR WASH

Cars can get pretty dirty from all that time on the road. Lather up with these facts about car washes.

AVERAGE PRICE OF AUTOMATIC CAR WASH:
$6-$9

CARS WASHED EVERY DAY:
8 million

CARS WASHED EVERY YEAR:
2.3 billion

WATER USED
TO WASH A CAR
BY HAND WITH A HOSE:

80-100
gallons
(303–379 l)

WATER USED
TO WASH A CAR AT
AN AUTOMATIC CAR WASH:

38
gallons
(144 l)

Busiest Car Wash Days

TUESDAY-THURSDAY:
31%

SATURDAY:
25%

FRIDAY:
20%

SUNDAY:
12%

MONDAY:
12%

STRAIGHT-A STUDIERS

How much time do you spend on homework?
See how your study time compares to that of kids across the country.

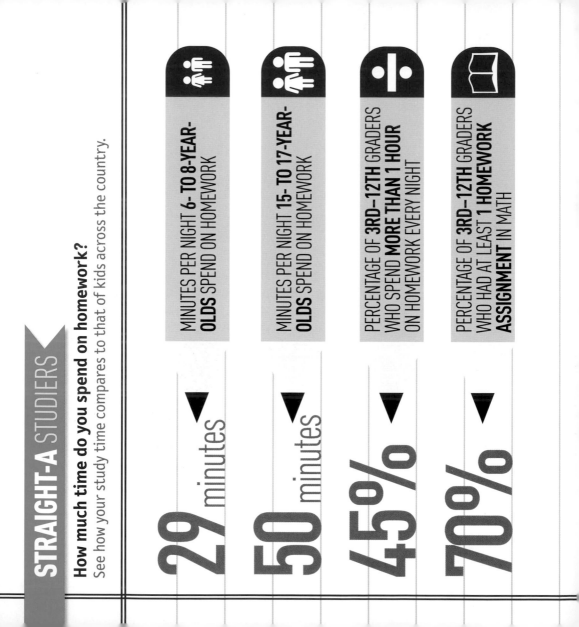

29 minutes ▼ — MINUTES PER NIGHT **6- TO 8-YEAR-OLDS** SPEND ON HOMEWORK

50 minutes ▼ — MINUTES PER NIGHT **15- TO 17-YEAR-OLDS** SPEND ON HOMEWORK

45% ▼ — PERCENTAGE OF **3RD–12TH** GRADERS WHO SPEND **MORE THAN 1 HOUR** ON HOMEWORK EVERY NIGHT

70% ▼ — PERCENTAGE OF **3RD–12TH** GRADERS WHO HAD AT LEAST **1 HOMEWORK ASSIGNMENT** IN MATH

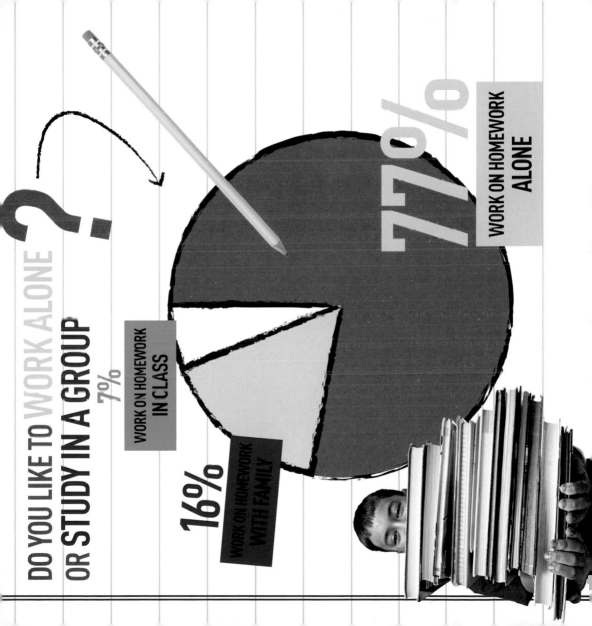

DO YOU LIKE TO WORK ALONE OR STUDY IN A GROUP

77% WORK ON HOMEWORK ALONE

7% WORK ON HOMEWORK IN CLASS

16% WORK ON HOMEWORK WITH FAMILY

There are almost **400,000** different beetles. That's about **40%** of all known insect species!

SOME RHINOCEROS BEETLES CAN LIFT UP TO

100 TIMES

THEIR OWN WEIGHT.

THAT'S LIKE A TEN-YEAR-OLD LIFTING A

6,000-POUND

(2,722-kg)

PICKUP TRUCK!

SUGAR SURPRISE

Cereal is a favorite at the breakfast table: 90% of American families have cereal in the pantry. But is this breakfast classic all it's cracked up to be? Before you chow down, learn more about the sugary surprise hidden in some cereal bowls.

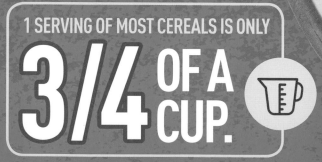

SOME CEREALS HAVE MORE THAN

15 GRAMS OF SUGAR

PER SERVING.

1 SERVING OF MOST CEREALS IS ONLY

3/4 OF A CUP.

SOME BOWLS CAN HOLD MORE THAN

2 CUPS OF CEREAL,

SO YOU COULD BE EATING MORE THAN

33 GRAMS OF SUGAR

PER BOWL.

THAT'S LIKE EATING MORE THAN

6 CHOCOLATE CHIP COOKIES

FOR BREAKFAST!

SPECIAL SPECIES

As the world's human population grows, it gets harder for some creatures to survive. According to the International Union for Conservation of Nature Red List of Threatened Species, almost 20,000 animals and plants are currently threatened with extinction. Here's a look at some endangered species around the globe.

RED WOLF:
250
REMAINING

LOGGERHEAD SEA TURTLE:
UP TO
67,000
NESTING FEMALES REMAINING

BLUE WHALE:
UP TO
25,000
REMAINING

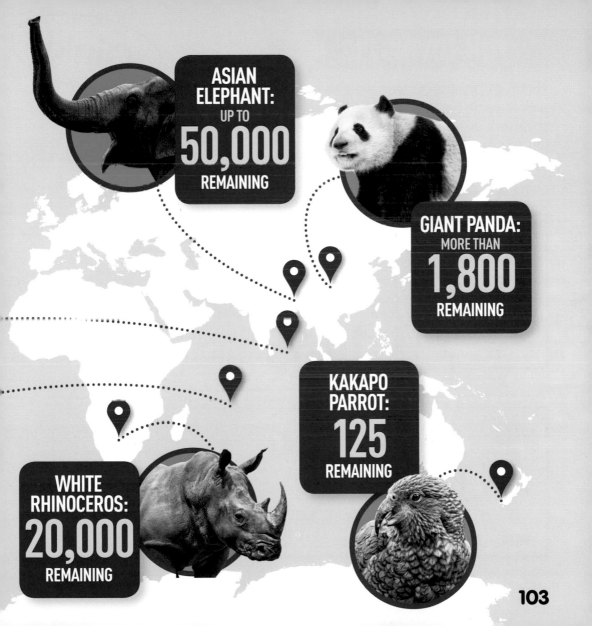

ASIAN ELEPHANT:
UP TO
50,000
REMAINING

GIANT PANDA:
MORE THAN
1,800
REMAINING

KAKAPO PARROT:
125
REMAINING

WHITE RHINOCEROS:
20,000
REMAINING

103

THE **FUN-LOVING PIG**

Here, piggy piggy! With more than **one billion** pigs roaming Earth at a time, these smart, social creatures are one of the most populous on the entire planet. Meet the playful pig!

TEETH:
44

LIFE SPAN:
10-15 YEARS

FEET:
4 LEGS
WITH **4 HOOFED TOES** ON EACH FOOT

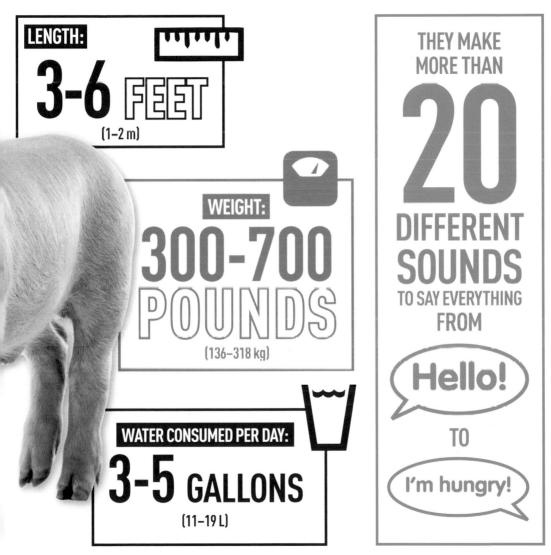

LENGTH:

3-6 FEET
(1–2 m)

WEIGHT:

300-700 POUNDS
(136–318 kg)

WATER CONSUMED PER DAY:

3-5 GALLONS
(11–19 L)

THEY MAKE MORE THAN

20

DIFFERENT SOUNDS
TO SAY EVERYTHING FROM

Hello!

TO

I'm hungry!

850 MILLION

PEOPLE VISIT MUSEUMS EVERY YEAR.

THAT'S MORE THAN ATTENDANCE AT ALL MAJOR SPORTING EVENTS COMBINED!

SUBJECT STANDINGS

What's your favorite class in school?

Researchers surveyed kids to find out their picks for #1 school subjects. Find out where your favorite class clocks in!

Students have been taking math tests for centuries! Researchers believe that ancient Egyptians used arithmetic, algebra, and geometry as far back as **3000 B.C.**

SOCIAL

PHYSICAL EDUCATION 8%

MATH

MUSIC 5%   **ART 5%**

SCIENCE 14%

STUDIES 10%

FOREIGN LANGUAGE 3%

ENGLISH 10%

23%

OTHER 8%

COMPUTERS 3%

THEATRE/DANCE 2%

Kids who study art are **4 TIMES** more likely to get good grades and **3 TIMES** more likely to have good attendance.

REPTILE SMACKDOWN

These two reptiles share the same scaly skin and terrifying teeth, but what sets them apart? It's a cold-blooded battle!

AMERICAN ALLIGATOR

WEIGHT: UP TO **1,000** POUNDS (454 kg)

BITE **FORCE:** 2,125 POUNDS PER SQUARE INCH (149 kg/sq cm)

FASTEST SPEED ON LAND: **9** MILES AN HOUR (15 km/h)

NUMBER OF TEETH: **80**

TOTAL BODY LENGTH: **11-15** FEET (3–4.5 m)

AVERAGE LIFE SPAN: **30-50** YEARS

SALTWATER CROCODILE

WEIGHT: UP TO **2,200** POUNDS
(998 kg)

BITE

FORCE: **3,700 POUNDS** PER SQUARE INCH
(260 kg/sq cm)

That's the strongest bite ever measured! When you eat a steak, you're biting with about **150 POUNDS** PER SQUARE INCH.
(10.5 kg/sq cm)

FASTEST SPEED ON LAND:

11 MILES AN HOUR (18 km/h)

NUMBER OF TEETH: **64-68**

TOTAL BODY LENGTH: up to **23** FEET (7 m)

WINNER!

AVERAGE LIFE SPAN: **70-100 YEARS**

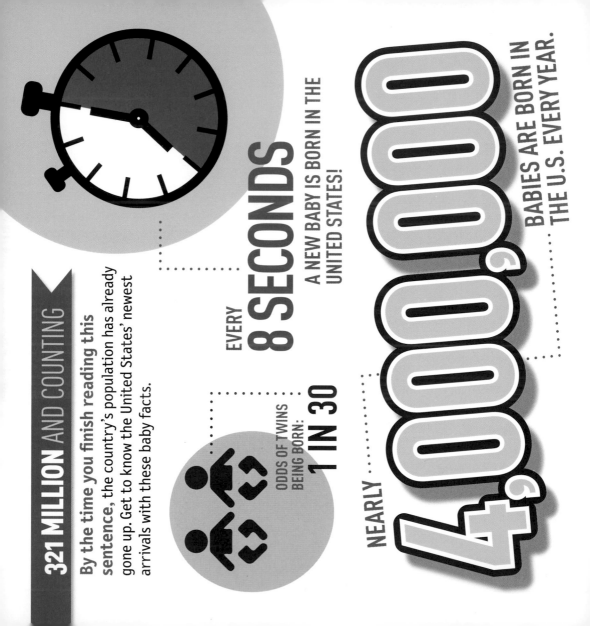

321 MILLION AND COUNTING

By the time you finish reading this **sentence**, the country's population has already gone up. Get to know the United States' newest arrivals with these baby facts.

EVERY
8 SECONDS
A NEW BABY IS BORN IN THE UNITED STATES!

ODDS OF TWINS BEING BORN:
1 IN 30

NEARLY
4,000,000
BABIES ARE BORN IN THE U.S. EVERY YEAR.

BOYS VS. GIRLS:

BOY BABIES HAVE OUTNUMBERED GIRL BABIES IN THE U.S. FOR THE LAST 60 YEARS.

51% OF BABIES BORN IN THE U.S. ARE BOYS.

49% OF BABIES BORN IN THE U.S. ARE GIRLS.

NUMBER OF BONES A BABY HAS AT BIRTH: AROUND **300**

NUMBER OF BONES AN ADULT HAS: **206**

BY 5 MONTHS OLD, A BABY IS **2 TIMES HEAVIER** THAN AT BIRTH. AT THAT RATE, THE BABY WOULD WEIGH AROUND **250 POUNDS** (113 kg) BY AGE 2!

What color are your eyes? Are they blue, gray, brown, green, or somewhere in between? See how your eye color compares to others in the United States with this awesome optical chart.

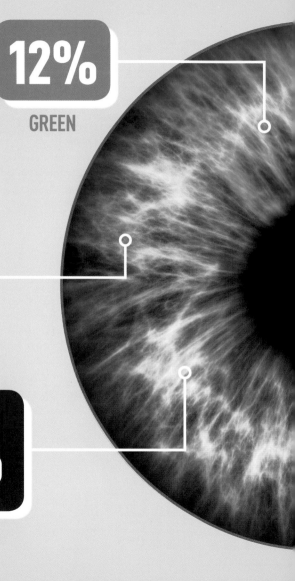

12%
GREEN

15%
GRAY OR HAZEL

16%
BROWN

32%
BLUE

25%
DARK BROWN

So far, scientists have found approximately **16 GENES** that help determine our eye color.

GOT SPACE JUNK?

Look up in the sky. Are those stars you see? Look again! It could be space junk. More than 500,000 pieces of man-made debris are currently floating around Earth. What's up there, and where did it come from? Read on to find out.

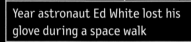

1965

Year astronaut Ed White lost his glove during a space walk

20,000+

Pieces of debris larger than a softball orbiting Earth

MILLIONS

Pieces of debris that are so small they can't be tracked

500 MILES (805 km)

Distance most space junk
floats above Earth's surface

17,500 MPH (7,823 m/s)

Speed that objects travel through space. At this
high speed, even the tiniest piece of junk can be a
serious hazard. Space shuttle windows have been
damaged by pieces as small as a fleck of paint!

500,000

Pieces of debris the size
of a marble or larger

9

Number of telescopes the United States Air Force
uses to track each and every object floating in space

NATIONAL PARK NUMBERS

Ever since the first national park was created by President Ulysses S. Grant in 1872, Americans have traveled far and wide to see the most spectacular sites in the country. Take a tour through America's most visited national parks.

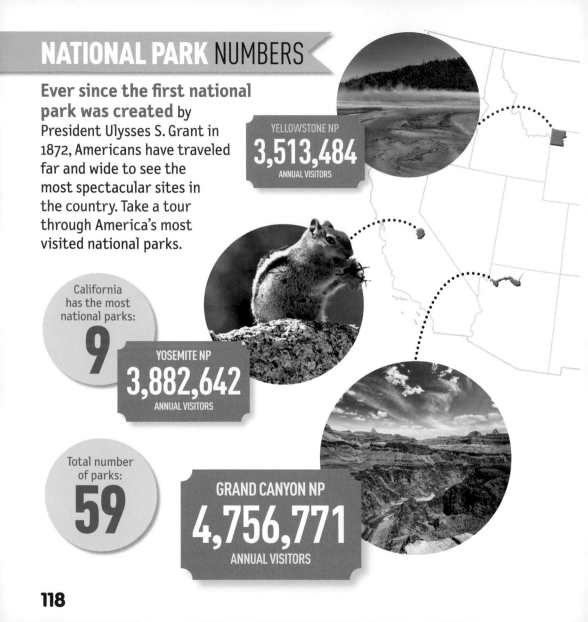

YELLOWSTONE NP
3,513,484
ANNUAL VISITORS

California has the most national parks:
9

YOSEMITE NP
3,882,642
ANNUAL VISITORS

Total number of parks:
59

GRAND CANYON NP
4,756,771
ANNUAL VISITORS

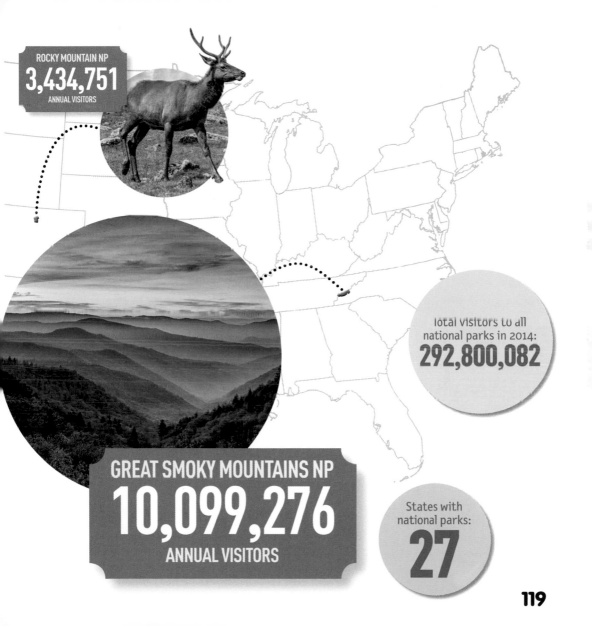

ROCKY MOUNTAIN NP
3,434,751
ANNUAL VISITORS

Total visitors to all national parks in 2014:
292,800,082

GREAT SMOKY MOUNTAINS NP
10,099,276
ANNUAL VISITORS

States with national parks:
27

A FLEA CAN JUMP MORE THAN

100 TIMES

ITS BODY LENGTH.

THAT'S LIKE A KID JUMPING TO THE TOP OF A

34-STORY

BUILDING.

ANIMAL BIRTHDAY BASH

How many candles were on your last birthday cake? While we count our lives in years, some insects count theirs in minutes, and other animals live long past 100! Bring a gift and get ready to learn more about average animal life spans.

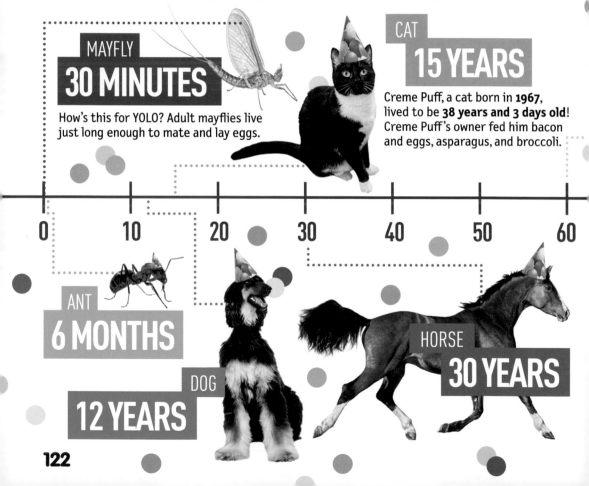

MAYFLY
30 MINUTES

How's this for YOLO? Adult mayflies live just long enough to mate and lay eggs.

CAT
15 YEARS

Creme Puff, a cat born in **1967**, lived to be **38 years and 3 days old**! Creme Puff's owner fed him bacon and eggs, asparagus, and broccoli.

0   10   20   30   40   50   60

ANT
6 MONTHS

DOG
12 YEARS

HORSE
30 YEARS

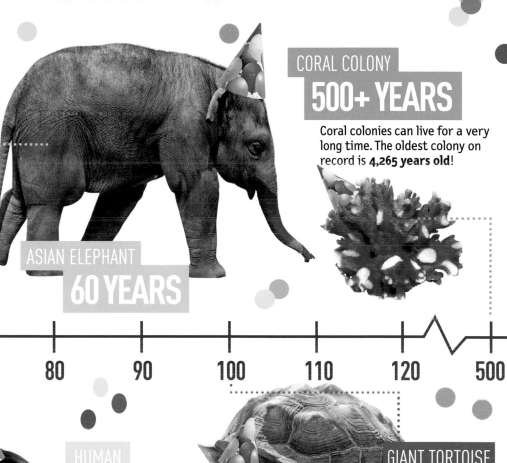

CORAL COLONY
500+ YEARS

Coral colonies can live for a very long time. The oldest colony on record is **4,265 years old**!

ASIAN ELEPHANT
60 YEARS

| 70 | 80 | 90 | 100 | 110 | 120 | 500 |

HUMAN
71 YEARS

71 candles is just the beginning! The world's oldest person lived to celebrate her **122nd birthday**.

GIANT TORTOISE
100+ YEARS

Jonathan, a giant tortoise living in Seychelles, is **183 years old**. He's the oldest animal in the world!

123

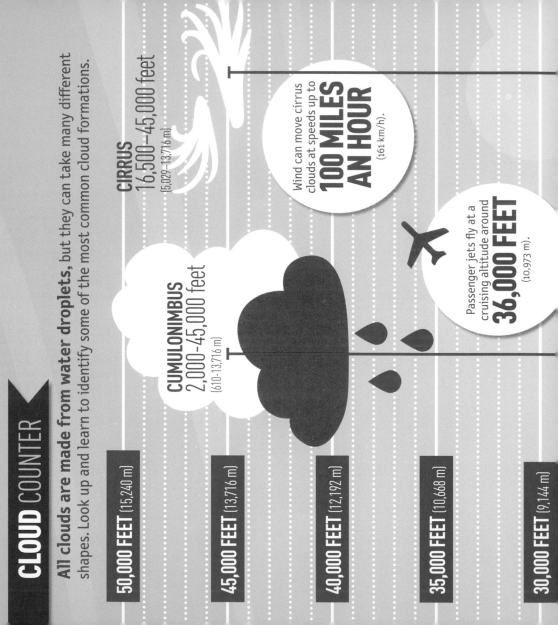

CLOUD COUNTER

All clouds are made from water droplets, but they can take many different shapes. Look up and learn to identify some of the most common cloud formations.

CIRRUS
16,500–45,000 feet
(5,029–13,716 m)

CUMULONIMBUS
2,000–45,000 feet
(610–13,716 m)

Wind can move cirrus clouds at speeds up to **100 MILES AN HOUR** (161 km/h).

Passenger jets fly at a cruising altitude around **36,000 FEET** (10,973 m).

50,000 FEET (15,240 m)

45,000 FEET (13,716 m)

40,000 FEET (12,192 m)

35,000 FEET (10,668 m)

30,000 FEET (9,144 m)

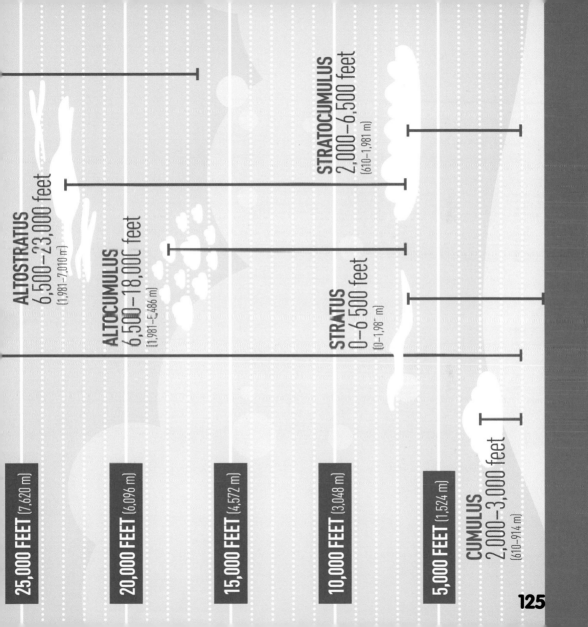

ALTOSTRATUS
6,500–23,000 feet
(1,981–7,010 m)

ALTOCUMULUS
6,500–18,000 feet
(1,981–5,486 m)

STRATOCUMULUS
2,000–6,500 feet
(610–1,981 m)

STRATUS
0–6,500 feet
(0–1,981 m)

CUMULUS
2,000–3,000 feet
(610–914 m)

25,000 FEET (7,620 m)

20,000 FEET (6,096 m)

15,000 FEET (4,572 m)

10,000 FEET (3,048 m)

5,000 FEET (1,524 m)

125

SENSE STATS

Our five senses help us experience the world through sight, smell, touch, taste, and sound. Here are some mind-blowing facts about our incredible senses.

ABOUT
30%
OF NEURONS IN THE BRAIN'S CORTEX ARE DEDICATED TO VISION.

YOUR NOSE CAN DETECT
1 TRILLION
DIFFERENT SCENTS.

80%
OF WHAT WE EXPERIENCE AS TASTE IS ACTUALLY SMELL.

WE ARE BORN
WITH APPROXIMATELY

3,500

INNER EAR CELLS THAT
HELP US HEAR SOUNDS.

That's one of the
densest areas of touch
receptors in the

WHOLE
BODY!

NUMBER OF TOUCH
RECEPTORS IN EACH FINGERTIP:

3,000

WHAT'S YOUR FAVORITE COLOR?

Do you have a favorite hue? A sociologist asked adults to pick their favorite color and charted their answers. The results may surprise you!

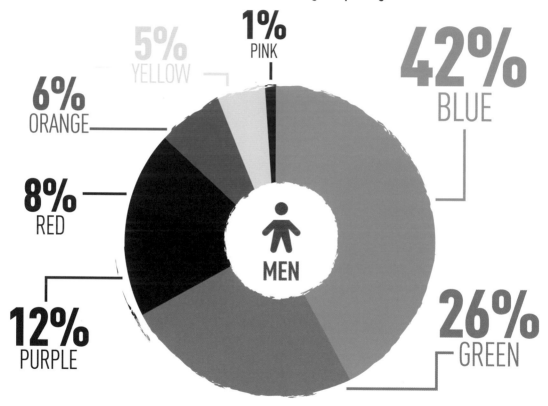

1%
PINK

5%
YELLOW

6%
ORANGE

42%
BLUE

8%
RED

MEN

12%
PURPLE

26%
GREEN

FOR MEN, THE WINNER IS BLUE!

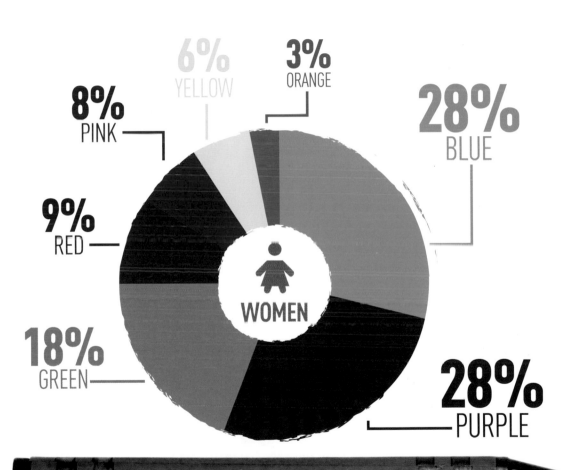

6%
YELLOW

3%
ORANGE

8%
PINK

28%
BLUE

9%
RED

WOMEN

18%
GREEN

28%
PURPLE

WOMEN LIKE BLUE, TOO, BUT IT'S TIED WITH PURPLE.

RIGHTY OR LEFTY?

When you go to write your name or throw a ball, which hand do you use? Do you have a favorite side? Studies show that one hand is more commonly used than the other. See how you compare with the rest of the world in this handy breakdown.

<1%
OF PEOPLE ARE AMBIDEXTROUS, MEANING THEY CAN USE BOTH HANDS.

LEFTY

10%
OF PEOPLE ARE LEFT-HANDED.

About **30 MILLION** people in the United States are left-handed.

RIGHTY

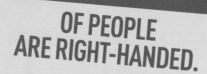

90%

OF PEOPLE ARE RIGHT-HANDED.

Ever since Jacob Davis and Levi Strauss patented their pant design in 1873, classic American blue jeans have become famous around the world. Put on your favorite pair and learn more about this fashion icon.

96% OF AMERICANS OWN A PAIR OF JEANS.

AVERAGE PAIRS OF JEANS A MAN OWNS: **6**

AVERAGE PAIRS OF JEANS A WOMAN OWNS: **7**

MORE THAN 50% OF DENIM IS MADE IN ASIA, MOSTLY IN CHINA, INDIA, AND BANGLADESH.

AVERAGE PRICE OF A PAIR OF JEANS:

$45.32

HERE'S WHAT MAKES UP

1 PAIR
OF LEVI'S JEANS:

6 RIVETS

5 BUTTONS

3.5 YARDS (3 M) FABRIC

1 RED LOGO TAG

EACH YEAR,

2.5 ACRES

OF TREES

(1 ha)

PRODUCE ENOUGH OXYGEN FOR

45
PEOPLE

TO BREATHE FOR A YEAR.

"I AM **FASCINATED BY HOW FLEXIBLE DATA IS.** I LOVE HOW IT IS MULTIDIMENSIONAL. YOU CAN LOOK AT IT FROM MANY DIFFERENT ANGLES AND **ASK IT DIFFERENT QUESTIONS** ... OR THE SAME QUESTION IN DIFFERENT WAYS. IT'S MY JOB TO FIND THE BEST WAY TO EXPRESS **WHAT IS HIDDEN IN THE DATA.**"

AN INTERVIEW WITH NICHOLAS FELTON

INFORMATION DESIGNER

Q: WHAT IS IT THAT YOU DO?
A: I am a designer. While I work with text and images like a traditional designer, I really enjoy working with data. My projects tend to be based on sets of data that are given to me by clients or that I collect myself. The challenge as a designer is to translate this information into a graphic form that communicates the essence of the data set to someone else.

Q: HOW DOES YOUR WORK HELP OTHERS?
A: I also build applications to help people gather data and use it to communicate or understand themselves. I want to give people simple tools for collecting and investigating data.

Q: WHAT'S THE SECRET TO BEING A SUCCESSFUL DATA DESIGNER?
A: I have learned the most by making things that no one asked me to do. The more you make things, the better you get ... so if you find a passion for working with data, then pursue that passion in school, at home, on vacation ... whenever inspiration or opportunity presents itself!

The background of this page is data visualization by Felton.

137

SOIL STATS

Look around your garden and you'll see lots of living things: pretty flowers, chirping birds, and more. But did you know there's a whole living world hidden in the soil beneath your feet? Next time you dig in the dirt, think about these fascinating facts!

9 FEET [3 m]
FUNGI STRANDS

30 EARTHWORMS
Dig around in the dirt and you'll find up to

per square foot (0.09 sq m). They break down organic matter in the soil.

1 TEASPOON
OF SOIL CONTAINS:

100
TINY SOIL INSECTS

HUNDREDS
CILIATES & NEMATODES

SEVERAL THOUSAND
FLAGELLATES & AMOEBAS

UP TO 1 BILLION
BACTERIA

There can be as much as **4,000 POUNDS** (1,814 kg) of plant roots in every acre (4,047 sq m) of soil.

BIG **BABIES**

Have you ever met a 250-pound (113-kg) **baby?**
Some of these animals' beloved bundles are just plain
huge! Bring a supersized bottle and get ready to
meet some of the world's biggest babies.

Polar bears are
born small, but these
babies grow fast! By 8
months old, a baby polar
bear weighs nearly

100 pounds

(45 kg).

7.5
POUNDS

(3.4 kg)

baby human

60
POUNDS

(27 kg)

baby hippo

150
POUNDS

(68 kg)

baby giraffe

200
POUNDS

(91 kg)

Baby elephants
depend on their
moms for the first
2-3 YEARS
of their lives.

baby elephant

VOLCANIC STATS

Deep below Earth's surface, pressure is building in pools of hot liquid rock and gas called magma. When the pressure builds, magma bursts up through the world's volcanoes. More than 80 percent of Earth's surface was formed by these eruptions. Explore this map of the world's most active volcanic areas and learn some explosive facts along the way.

▲ Symbol for a volcano

1,500
Number of potentially active volcanoes on Earth

2,000°F (1,093° C)
Maximum temperature of molten lava flowing from erupting volcano

33

Number of years Kilauea in Hawaii has been continuously erupting. It's one of the most active volcanoes on Earth!

169

Number of active volcanoes in the United States

75%

Percent of Earth's volcanoes located in the Ring of Fire around the Pacific Ocean

22,563 FEET (6,877 m)

Height of Ojos del Salado in the Andes mountains, the world's highest active volcano

500

Number of historically recorded volcanic eruptions

NUTRIENT NUMBERS

We all know fruits and vegetables are good for us, but which one is the healthiest of all? Scientists compared 47 different foods and calculated their Nutrient Density Score to find out which one packs the most powerful nutrient punch. Check out their results below!

11 SWEET POTATO

11 BLACKBERRY

19 LEMON

20 TOMATO

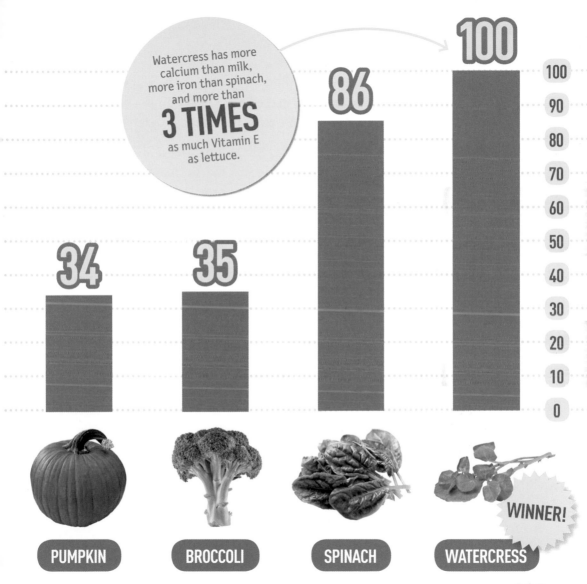

Watercress has more calcium than milk, more iron than spinach, and more than **3 TIMES** as much Vitamin E as lettuce.

34 — PUMPKIN

35 — BROCCOLI

86 — SPINACH

100 — WATERCRESS

WINNER!

COUNTING SNOWFLAKES

Yay! It's a snow day! You've gone sledding at the best hills and built a mighty fine snowman, but do you know just how many flakes fall from the sky each winter? Put on your mittens and learn more about snow with these frozen facts.

U.S. record for most snowfall in 24 hours:

75.8 INCHES
(1.9 m)

Silver Lake, Colorado—April 14–15, 1921

The biggest snowflake on record was

15 INCHES
(38 cm) wide.

MORE THAN

1,000,000,000,000,000,000,000,000

SNOWFLAKES FALL EVERY WINTER.

What's that big number? It's

10^{24}

or one septillion!

Tallest snowperson ever built:

122 FEET 1 INCH

(37.21 m)

Built by people in Bethel, Maine, over 1 month in 2008

OUTNUMBERED

FOR EVERY HUMAN, THERE ARE

1.4 BI

LLION

INSECTS ALIVE RIGHT NOW.

To show that many insects, it would take **20 MILLION** pages full of bugs just like this one!

GAME GRAPHS

In decades past, video games used to be stuck in arcades. Today, we can game anywhere, anytime! With high-tech mobile phones and video game consoles available worldwide, more people are discovering the fun of gaming every year. Here's a look at how many people are plugging in.

155 MILLION
AMERICANS PLAY VIDEO GAMES.

42%
PLAY REGULARLY.

51%
OF HOUSEHOLDS OWN
A GAME CONSOLE.

79%
OF PARENTS PLACE TIME LIMITS
ON VIDEO GAME PLAYING.

GAME GEAR
Top Devices Gamers Use to Play Games

SMARTPHONE

+ 56%
GAME CONSOLE

62%
PC

35%

21%
HANDHELD GAME

TOP **3** TYPES OF VIDEO GAMES:

31%	30%	30%
SOCIAL GAMES	ACTION GAMES	PUZZLE GAMES

THERE ARE

24.9 TRILLION

CELL COUNT

🔴 = 200 BILLION CELLS

RED BLOOD CELLS IN THE HUMAN BODY.

IT WOULD TAKE YOU 789,050 YEARS TO COUNT THEM ALL ONE BY ONE!

SAHARA STATS

The Sahara desert is one of the driest places on the planet.
Let's take a trip to Africa—don't forget your sunscreen!

TEMPERATURE:

122°F
(50°C)

SIZE:

3,300,000 SQUARE MILES (8,546,960 sq km)

COVERAGE:

8%
OF THE WORLD'S LAND AREA

THE CONTINENTAL UNITED STATES WOULD FIT INSIDE IT WITH ROOM TO SPARE!

LOCATION:

COVERS MOST OF NORTH AFRICA, SPREADING ACROSS

11 AFRICAN COUNTRIES:

LIBYA, ALGERIA, EGYPT, TUNISIA, CHAD, MOROCCO, ERITREA, NIGER, MAURITANIA, MALI, AND THE SUDAN

RAINFALL: LESS THAN **3 INCHES** (8 cm) PER YEAR

THAT'S AS TALL AS **2 STATUES OF LIBERTY** STACKED ON TOP OF EACH OTHER!

600 FEET [183 m]

HEIGHT: SAND DUNES CAN RISE AS HIGH AS

For thousands of years, gold has been a symbol of wealth. But gold is more than just a sparkly luxury. Here's the scoop on the many ways we use this precious metal.

10%
MONEY

12%
ELECTRONICS

Precious metals like gold, silver, and copper have been used as currency for more than

6,000 YEARS.

Today, gold coins and bars are bought as an investment.

Gold melts at

1948°F
(1,064°C).

Gold is a great conductor of electricity and is found in many of your favorite tech gadgets. Cell phones have an average of **50 CENTS'** worth of gold inside.

174,000 TONS
(157,850 t)
of gold have been mined by humans.

78% JEWELRY

Scientists think the gold in Earth's crust came from asteroid impacts about **4 BILLION YEARS AGO.**

MAN'S **BEST FRIEND**

Did you know that more than 70 million pet dogs live in American homes? That's a lot of furry friends! With more than 180 different dog breeds recognized by the American Kennel Club, there's a perfect pet for every family. Here's a look at the ten most popular pooches in the United States.

#8 Poodle

#4 Bulldog

#9 Rottweiler

#5 Beagle

#10 Boxer

#7 Yorkshire Terrier

#6 French Bulldog

#2

German Shepherd

#3

Golden Retriever

#1

Labrador Retriever

THE LABRADOR RETRIEVER HAS BEEN THE MOST POPULAR DOG BREED IN AMERICA FOR THE PAST

25 Years!

YUM!

1
BAT

CAN EAT UP TO

1,000

MOSQUITOES

EVERY HOUR.

NOT-SO-DISTANT RELATIVES

Do you have any chimpanzee cousins?
How about a fruit fly? Believe it or not, all
living things on Earth—animals, plants, and
fungi—share a common ancestor that lived
1.6 billion years ago. Here's how much DNA
humans share with other organisms.

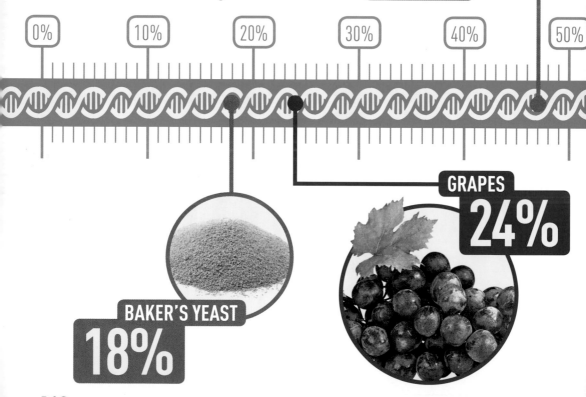

FRUIT FLY
47%

GRAPES
24%

BAKER'S YEAST
18%

0%   10%   20%   30%   40%   50%

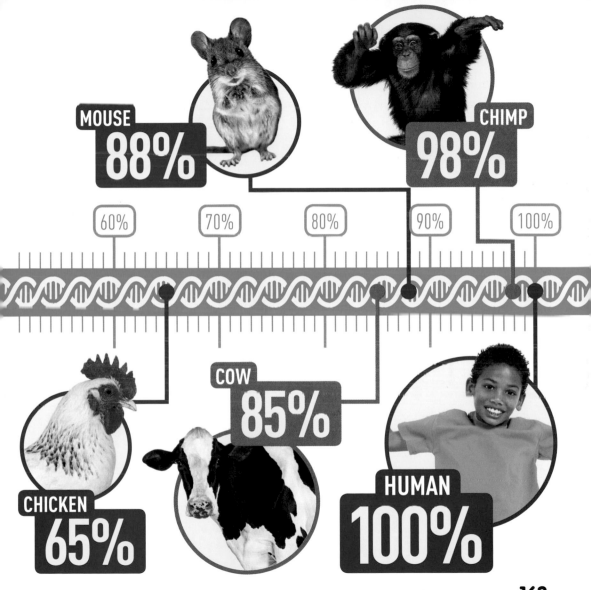

MOUSE
88%

CHIMP
98%

60% 70% 80% 90% 100%

CHICKEN
65%

COW
85%

HUMAN
100%

163

SUMMER STATISTICS

Ah, summer. Time to relax in the backyard, fire up the grill, and enjoy the warm weather. Soak up these fun summer facts!

EARTH'S AXIS TILTS AT
23.5°,
CHANGING THE PLANET'S ANGLE RELATIVE TO THE SUN (AND OUR WEATHER!).

THE SUN IS MORE THAN
94 MILLION
MILES (151 million km) FROM EARTH DURING THE SUMMER SOLSTICE.

FIRST DAY OF SUMMER IN THE NORTHERN HEMISPHERE:
JUNE 20 OR 21

FIRST DAY OF SUMMER IN THE SOUTHERN HEMISPHERE:
DECEMBER 21 OR 22

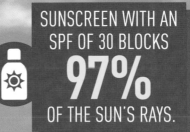

SUNSCREEN WITH AN SPF OF 30 BLOCKS **97%** OF THE SUN'S RAYS.

PERCENTAGE OF AMERICANS WHO SAY THEY KNOW HOW TO SWIM: **80%**

SYDNEY, AUSTRALIA, ENJOYS MORE THAN **340** SUNNY DAYS PER YEAR.

LONGEST BEACH IN THE WORLD: PRAIA DO CASSINO, BRAZIL ABOUT **150 MILES LONG** (241 km)

TONGUE-TIED

Can you lick your elbow? How about your eyelids? Well, you might not be able to, but these animals use their long tongues to lick, catch, and even smell their way through the day. Take a look at how these tongues measure up.

human
4
INCHES
(10 cm)

red-bellied woodpecker
6.7
INCHES
(17 cm)

aardvark
12
INCHES
(30.5 cm)

giraffe
20
INCHES
(51 cm)

anteater
24
INCHES
(61 cm)

veiled chameleon
36
INCHES
(91 cm)

The sun doesn't look that big when it's up in the sky,
but in reality, this fiery star is massive. In fact, it's 109 times
bigger than Earth! What's that look like? Let's find out!

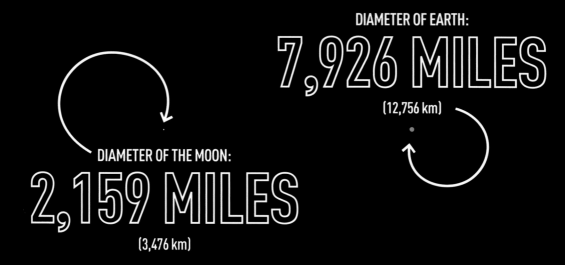

DIAMETER OF EARTH:

7,926 MILES

(12,756 km)

DIAMETER OF THE MOON:

2,159 MILES

(3,476 km)

THE SUN IS SO BIG THAT **1,300,000** EARTHS COULD FIT INSIDE IT.

DIAMETER OF THE SUN:

864,950 MILES

(1,392,002 km)

THE SUN WEIGHS **330,000** TIMES AS MUCH AS EARTH.

HOW TO MAKE A DIAMOND

These sparkly gems have been treasured for thousands of years, but geologists still aren't exactly sure how diamonds formed on Earth. Here's how scientists think natural diamonds are made.

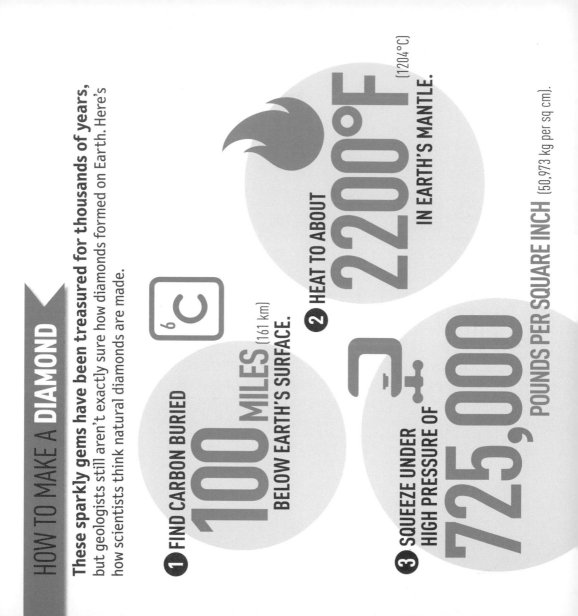

^{6}C

➊ FIND CARBON BURIED

100 MILES [161 km]

BELOW EARTH'S SURFACE.

➋ HEAT TO ABOUT

2200°F [1204°C]

IN EARTH'S MANTLE.

➌ SQUEEZE UNDER HIGH PRESSURE OF

725,000

POUNDS PER SQUARE INCH [50,973 kg per sq cm].

4 WAIT

1-3 BILLION YEARS

THAT'S ALMOST 75% OF THE AGE OF EARTH!

The largest rough diamond was discovered in **1905** and weighed **1.4 POUNDS** (635 g).

5 CUT RAW STONE INTO THE CLASSIC DIAMOND SHAPE WITH

58 FACETS.

DON'T BLINK!

YOU BLINK
28,800
TIMES EACH DAY.

ALL THOSE BLINKS ADD UP! YOU SPEND

THAT'S ABOUT 1 HOUR AND 36 MINUTES A DAY!

10%

OF YOUR WAKING HOURS WITH YOUR EYES CLOSED.

173

WORLD RECORD WEATHER

Can you imagine a day when temperatures rose above 130°F (54°C)? How about getting 12 feet (4 m) of rainfall in just three days? Here are a few of the world's most unbelievable recorded weather events.

HIGHEST TEMPERATURE

134°F (56.7°C)

Where: Furnace Creek, California
When: August 10, 1913

LONGEST TORNADO PATH

219 MILES (352.4 km)

Where: Ellington, Missouri, to Princeton, Indiana
When: March 18, 1925

LONGEST DRY PERIOD

173 MONTHS

Where: Arica, Chile
When: October 1903–January 1918

HEAVIEST HAILSTONE

2.25 POUNDS (1 kg)

Where: Gopalganj, Bangladesh
When: April 14, 1986

MAXIMUM WIND GUST

253 MILES AN HOUR (113.2 m/s)

Where: Barrow Island, Australia
When: April 10, 1996

GREATEST 72-HOUR RAINFALL

154.72 INCHES (3.93 m)

Where: Cratère Commerson, La Réunion, Indian Ocean
When: February 24–26, 2007

LOWEST TEMPERATURE

-128.5°F

Where: Vostok, Antarctica (-89.2°C)
When: July 21, 1983

YOSEMITE'S
HALF DOME ROCK
FORMATION IS

4,700 FEET

(1,433 m)

THAT'S A TENT!

EL CAPITAN

Measuring more than 3,000 feet (914 m) **tall,** El Capitan (Spanish for "the captain") is the largest block of granite rock in the world. The face of the formation is so sheer that only experienced rock climbers are allowed to scale it.

YOSEMITE SIGHTS

ABOVE THE VALLEY FLOOR.

YOSEMITE HAS

1,200

(3 108 sq km)

SQUARE MILES OF LAND.

YOSEMITE IS OPEN

365 DAYS A YEAR.

YOU CAN HIKE THROUGH

840 MILES

(1,352 km)

OF TRAILS IN THE PARK.

1 CAN OF SODA CONTAINS 40 GRAMS OF SUGAR.

THAT'S LIKE EATING **16** SUGAR CUBES.

Have you ever wondered what's at the center of Earth? Let's peel back the layers and take a peek!

Earth's interior is made of
4 LAYERS:
3 SOLID, 1 LIQUID.
The liquid outer core is made of molten metal that's nearly as hot as the sun!

Not to scale

	TEMPERATURE	DIAMETER/THICKNESS
INNER CORE	**9000–10,800°F** (5000–6000°C)	**1,500 miles** (2,414 km) **IN DIAMETER**

The inner core is hotter than any other part of the planet, but the pressure is so high the iron can't melt.

	TEMPERATURE	DIAMETER/THICKNESS
OUTER CORE	**7200–9000°F** (4000–5000°C)	**1,400 miles** (2,253 km) **THICK**

The liquid molten metal of the outer core creates Earth's magnetic field.

	TEMPERATURE	DIAMETER/THICKNESS
MANTLE	**930–7200°F** (500–4000°C)	**1,800 miles** (2,897 km) **THICK**

This rock is so hot, it flows like a thick liquid in slow-moving currents.

	TEMPERATURE	DIAMETER/THICKNESS
CRUST	**57–650°F** (14–1200°C)	**5-25 miles** (8–40 km) **THICK**

The mantle's moving magma currents have broken Earth's crust into pieces called plates. These plates float around very slowly. When these plates run into each other, mountains are formed.

THE TRUTH ABOUT TEETH

Just like us, animals use their teeth for biting, chomping, chewing, and gnawing. But you might be surprised to find out just how many teeth animals have! Sink your chompers into these sharp stats.

Elephant tusks are incisor teeth that never stop growing! The biggest tusk on record was more than **11 FEET** (3.5 m) long.

Your pet cat has the same number of teeth as the big cats in the wild: **30 TEETH.**

26 TEETH

30 TEETH

32 TEETH

42 TEETH

ELEPHANT **LION** **HUMAN** **DOG**

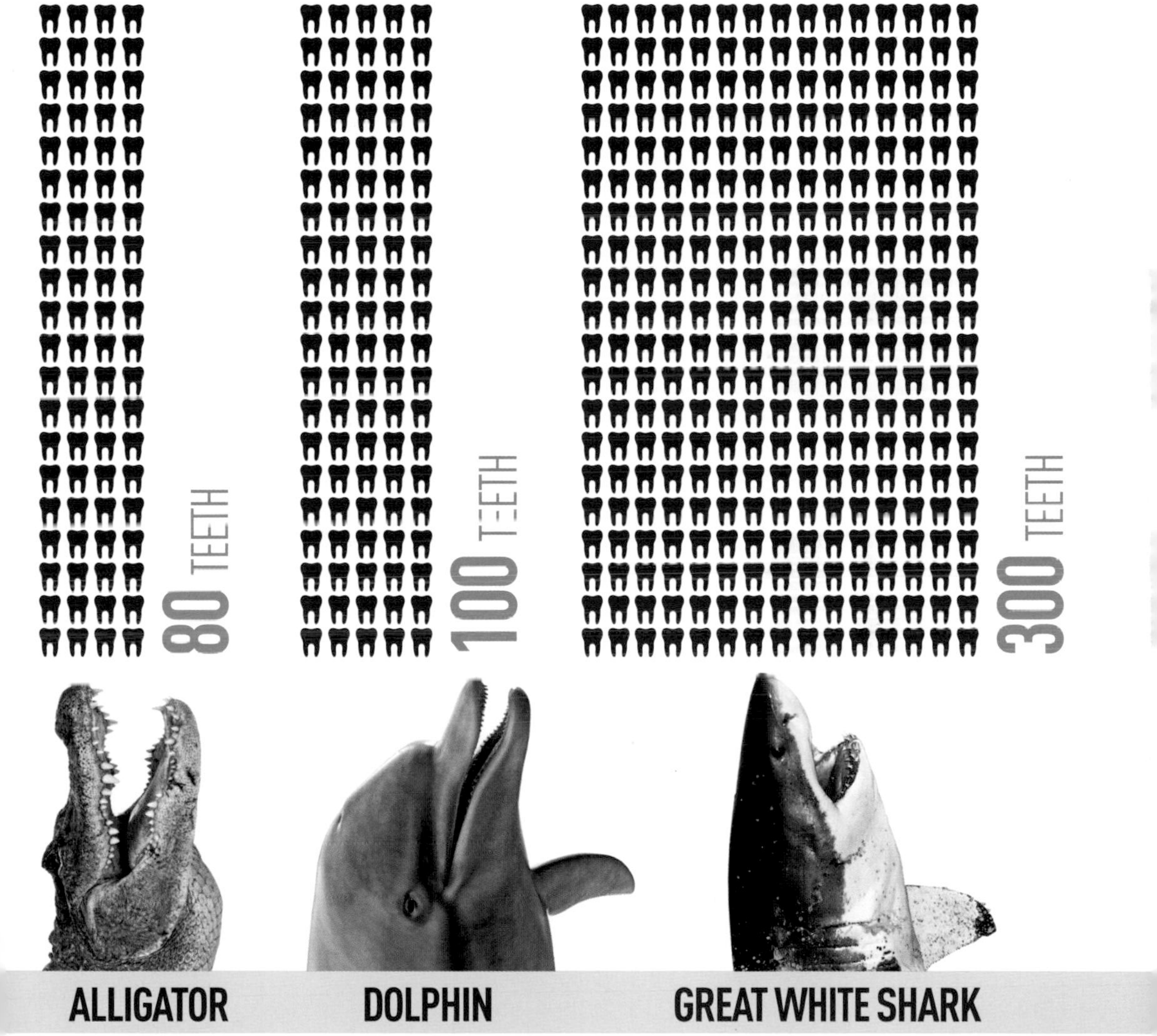

80 TEETH

100 TEETH

300 TEETH

ALLIGATOR

DOLPHIN

GREAT WHITE SHARK

ALASKA HAS
3 MILLION LAKES.
THAT MEANS THERE ARE NEARLY
4 TIMES
MORE LAKES THAN PEOPLE IN ALASKA!

⭐ Capital city
● Major city
◼ Lake

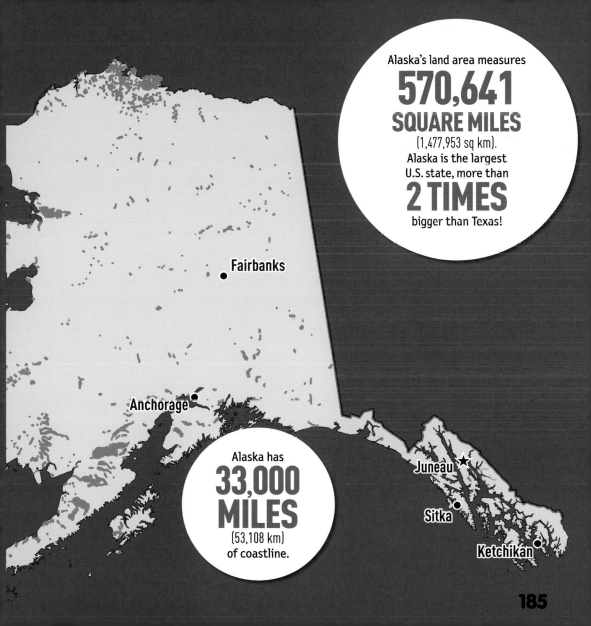

Alaska's land area measures
570,641
SQUARE MILES
(1,477,953 sq km).
Alaska is the largest
U.S. state, more than
2 TIMES
bigger than Texas!

Fairbanks

Anchorage

Alaska has
33,000
MILES
(53,108 km)
of coastline.

Juneau

Sitka

Ketchikan

TROPICAL TRENDS

This hot, humid biome can get more than 150 inches (381 cm) **of rainfall each year.** Covering less than 2 percent of Earth, it's home to 50 percent of the world's plants and animals. Without it, we wouldn't have coffee, cocoa, or many life-saving medicines. Welcome to the magical world of the tropical rain forest.

HEIGHT OF TALLEST TREES: **200 FEET** [61 m]

ANNUAL RAINFALL: **79-394 INCHES** [2-10 m]

28% OF THE WORLD'S OXYGEN IS MADE BY TREES IN THE RAIN FOREST.

MORE THAN **70%** OF CANCER-FIGHTING PLANTS COME FROM THE RAIN FOREST.

AND THERE COULD BE MANY MORE! LESS THAN **1%** OF RAIN FOREST PLANTS HAVE BEEN STUDIED.

50% OF ALL LIVING SPECIES ON EARTH ARE NATIVE TO RAIN FORESTS.

Yogurt is good for you and delicious, too. From fruity flavored yogurt to tangy Greek yogurt, this tasty treat is a breakfast favorite across the country—and around the world! Read on to learn more about this popular food.

34%
of all yogurt sold in the U.S. is Greek style.

The average American eats
14 POUNDS
(6 kg) of yogurt every year.

But that's nothing compared to people in Germany and France, who eat
60 POUNDS
(27 kg) of yogurt every year.

There are
17 GRAMS
of protein in one serving
of Greek yogurt.

**1
TEASPOON**
(5 ml) of yogurt
contains more than

420
MILLION
bacteria!

Don't get grossed out.
These are the good kind!
Probiotics, the healthy
bacteria found in yogurt,
boost our immune systems
and help us digest food.

Yogurt contains
2 MAIN
TYPES
of probiotics:
Lactobacillus bulgaricus
and *Streptococcus
thermophilus.*

FINGERPRINT FACTS

Take a look at your fingers. See anything special?
It's your fingerprint! This unique set of ridges and swirls is yours—and yours alone. Grab on to these fascinating fingerprint facts.

THE AVERAGE FINGERPRINT CAN HAVE AS MANY AS

150

INDIVIDUAL RIDGE CHARACTERISTICS.

YOUR FINGERPRINTS WERE THERE BEFORE YOU WERE BORN! A FETUS BEGINS DEVELOPING FINGERPRINTS AFTER

3 MONTHS

IN THE WOMB.

FINGERPRINTS HAVE BEEN USED TO CATCH CRIMINALS SINCE

200 B.C.

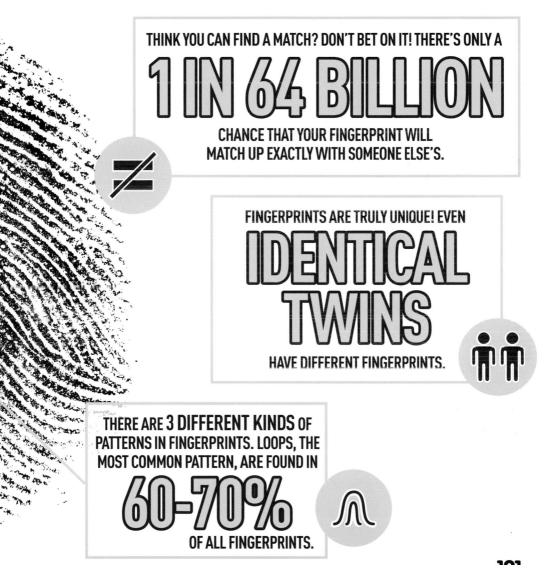

THINK YOU CAN FIND A MATCH? DON'T BET ON IT! THERE'S ONLY A

1 IN 64 BILLION

CHANCE THAT YOUR FINGERPRINT WILL
MATCH UP EXACTLY WITH SOMEONE ELSE'S.

FINGERPRINTS ARE TRULY UNIQUE! EVEN

IDENTICAL TWINS

HAVE DIFFERENT FINGERPRINTS.

THERE ARE **3 DIFFERENT KINDS** OF PATTERNS IN FINGERPRINTS. LOOPS, THE MOST COMMON PATTERN, ARE FOUND IN

60-70%

OF ALL FINGERPRINTS.

TIME FOR A **VACATION**

School's out! That means it's time for a fun trip. Pack your bags and get ready to hit the road with these American summer travel stats.

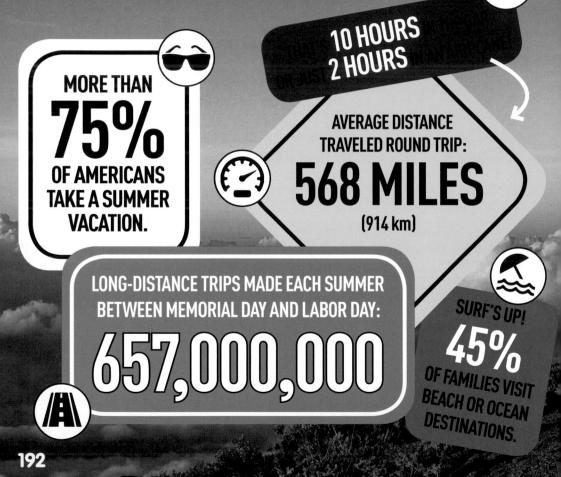

10 HOURS IN THE CAR
2 HOURS OR JUST IN AN AIRPLANE!

MORE THAN
75%
OF AMERICANS TAKE A SUMMER VACATION.

AVERAGE DISTANCE TRAVELED ROUND TRIP:
568 MILES
(914 km)

LONG-DISTANCE TRIPS MADE EACH SUMMER BETWEEN MEMORIAL DAY AND LABOR DAY:
657,000,000

SURF'S UP!
45%
OF FAMILIES VISIT BEACH OR OCEAN DESTINATIONS.

TOP VACATION STATES

10%
NEW YORK

9%
NORTH
CAROLINA

47%
OTHER
STATES

15%
CALIFORNIA

19%
FLORIDA

When's your birthday? How many other people share your special day? Find your birthday on the chart below to find out!

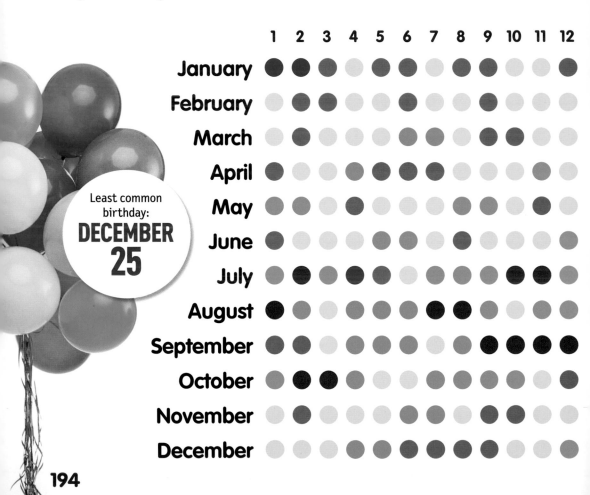

Least common birthday:
DECEMBER 25

194

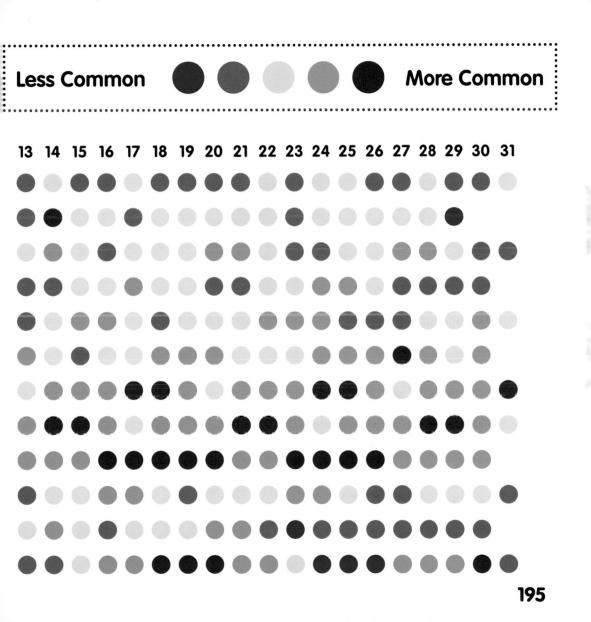

MEET **GIORGIA LUPI,** INFORMATION DESIGNER

NUMBERS CAN BE INFORMATIVE, AND BEAUTIFUL, TOO!

That's what information designer Giorgia Lupi believes. Blending the worlds of art and science, Giorgia uses design and data to help understand the world around us. Giorgia learned that data can help us understand people, too! For one year, Giorgia and her friend Stefanie collected data about their lives and created infographic art on postcards. Each week, the pair mailed their postcards to each other across the Atlantic Ocean, creating awesome data art and learning more about themselves—and their friendship!—in the process.

The background of this page shows some of the data art postcards made by Lupi.

WANT TO THINK LIKE A DATA DESIGNER?
HERE ARE GIORGIA'S TIPS!

1 THINK IN NUMBERS. DATA IS ALL AROUND US. OPEN YOUR EYES AND START LOOKING FOR DATA IN YOUR EVERYDAY LIFE!

2 PICK UP A PENCIL. I CAN'T THINK ABOUT A PROJECT WITHOUT A PEN AND SOME PAPER. GRAB A SKETCHBOOK AND START DRAWING. IT'LL HELP YOU UNDERSTAND YOUR SURROUNDINGS!

3 MAKE IT PRETTY. USE DESIGN AND COLOR TO MAKE YOUR INFOGRAPHICS POP. PEOPLE WILL SAY, "OH, THAT'S BEAUTIFUL. I WANT TO KNOW WHAT THIS IS ABOUT!"

GARBAGE PATCH FACTS

There's something gross swirling around the North Pacific Ocean. Ocean currents have collected a mass of trash into two giant floating landfills stretching from the west coast of North America all the way to Japan. Most of the garbage is plastic, which doesn't disintegrate when thrown away and is causing a big mess. Dive into the Great Pacific Garbage Patch and find out how you can help clean it up.

7.7 MILLION SQUARE MILES
(20 million sq km)

Total area of the ocean currents that contain the Great Pacific Garbage Patch

1.9 MILLION

Number of tiny pieces of plastic found per square mile (2.6 sq km) throughout the Garbage Patch. Most pieces are smaller than a grain of rice and float in the water, blocking sunlight from reaching the ecosystems below the surface.

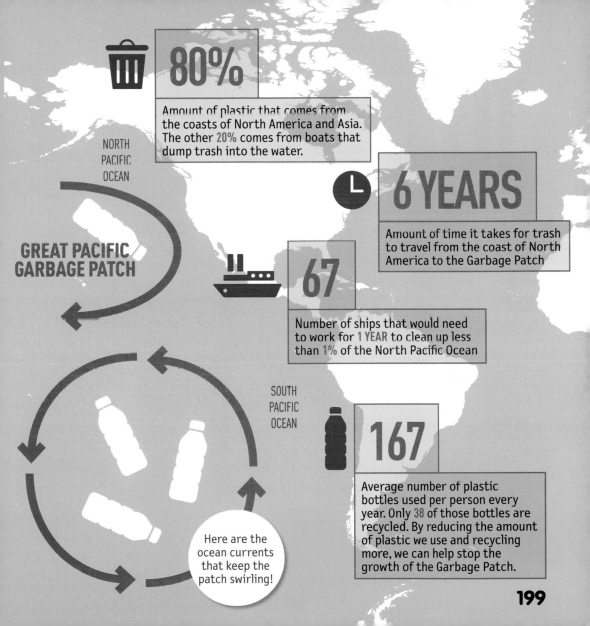

80%

Amount of plastic that comes from the coasts of North America and Asia. The other 20% comes from boats that dump trash into the water.

NORTH PACIFIC OCEAN

6 YEARS

Amount of time it takes for trash to travel from the coast of North America to the Garbage Patch

GREAT PACIFIC GARBAGE PATCH

67

Number of ships that would need to work for 1 YEAR to clean up less than 1% of the North Pacific Ocean

SOUTH PACIFIC OCEAN

167

Average number of plastic bottles used per person every year. Only 38 of those bottles are recycled. By reducing the amount of plastic we use and recycling more, we can help stop the growth of the Garbage Patch.

Here are the ocean currents that keep the patch swirling!

199

HEIGHT UP TO

10 FEET
(3 m)

STANDING ON
HIND LEGS

TAIL UP TO

5
INCHES (13 cm) LONG

WORLD
POPULATION

25,000
BEARS ROAM THE ARCTIC.

They may look cuddly, but polar bears are tough. Living in the coldest places on Earth—the Arctic ice sheets of Alaska, Canada, Russia, Greenland, and Norway—the polar bear has evolved to thrive in harsh conditions. Bundle up and step into the polar bear's frozen world.

SMELL RANGE

UP TO

20

MILES
(32 km)

SWIM RANGE

UP TO

200

MILES (322 km) FROM LAND

LIFE SPAN UP TO

30

YEARS

BODY UP TO

8

FEET (2 m) LONG

TOTAL WEIGHT UP TO

1,600

POUNDS (726 kg)

PAWS UP TO

12

INCHES (30 cm) WIDE

201

YOUR WATERY BODY

Did you know more than half your body is made of water? Here's a look at the H$_2$O inside you.

BRAIN

73%
WATER

BONES

31%
WATER

SKIN

64%
WATER

HEART

73%
WATER

KIDNEYS

79%
WATER

LUNGS

83%
WATER

PRIMATE SMACKDOWN

They may share a common ancestor, but these two simian relatives couldn't be more different. It's a battle of the primates!

HOW CAN YOU TELL THE DIFFERENCE BETWEEN AN APE AND A MONKEY? **LOOK FOR THE TAIL!** MOST MONKEYS HAVE TAILS, WHILE APES DON'T.

APES

EXAMPLES: **GORILLAS, CHIMPANZEES, ORANGUTANS, BONOBOS, EVEN HUMANS!**

CHIMPANZEES ARE OUR CLOSEST LIVING RELATIVES, SHARING **98%** OF OUR DNA.

WEIGHT: UP TO **485** POUNDS (220 kg)

HEIGHT: UP TO **6 FEET** (2 m)

MOVEMENT: CAN WALK ON **2 LEGS**

COOLEST FACT: CHIMPS ARE ONE OF THE FEW ANIMAL SPECIES KNOWN TO MAKE AND USE TOOLS.

MONKEYS

EXAMPLES:
BABOONS, MACAQUES

 WEIGHT: UP TO **77 POUNDS** (35 kg)

HEIGHT: UP TO **3 FEET** (91 cm)

MOVEMENT: MOSTLY WALK ON **4 LEGS**

COOLEST FACT: A HOWLER MONKEY'S LOUD ROAR CAN BE HEARD FROM **3 MILES** (5 km) AWAY.

SPIDER MONKEYS ARE SOCIAL, HANGING OUT IN LARGE GROUPS OF **24–36 MONKEYS** IN THE WILD.

DEAD SEA STATS

Between the countries of Jordan and Israel sits the Dead Sea, which is actually a very special lake. For thousands of years, the Dead Sea has attracted visitors from around the Mediterranean who seek out its salty waters. Learn what this destination is all about with these Dead Sea stats.

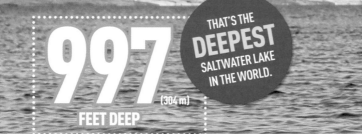

997
(304 m)

FEET DEEP

THAT'S THE **DEEPEST** SALTWATER LAKE IN THE WORLD.

There's magic in the water ... or so they say. Some people believe that the Dead Sea has healing properties.

WATER DENSITY:

77
(1,233 kg/m³)

POUNDS PER CUBIC FOOT

THAT MAKES SWIMMING IN THE DEAD SEA MORE LIKE **FLOATING.**

34% SALINITY

THAT'S **9 TIMES SALTIER** THAN THE OCEAN.

9 MILES WIDE (15 KM)

31 MILES LONG (50 km)

1,407 (429 m) FEET BELOW SEA LEVEL

THAT'S EARTH'S **LOWEST ELEVATION** ON LAND.

WHAT IF... YOU SWALLOWED A PIECE OF GUM?

Gum is sweet, chewy, bubbly fun. But what happens if you accidentally swallow a piece? Does it really stay in your stomach for seven years? Find out the truth below and learn more about this sweet treat.

AMOUNT OF CHEWING GUM SOLD PER YEAR IN THE UNITED STATES:
300,000 tons
(272,155 t)

VARIETIES OF GUM MADE AROUND THE WORLD:
OVER 1,000

AVERAGE CALORIES IN A STICK OF GUM:
5-10

GULP! YOU ACCIDENTALLY SWALLOW YOUR GUM. IT TAKES **2–3 SECONDS** TO GO DOWN YOUR ESOPHAGUS.

THE GUM MOVES INTO YOUR STOMACH, WHERE IT IS PARTIALLY DISSOLVED BY UP TO **3 OUNCES** (89 ml) OF STOMACH ACID.

AGE OF OLDEST PIECE OF GUM:
5,000 YEARS OLD

PERCENTAGE OF PEOPLE IN IRAN WHO CHEW GUM:
82%

Why? In Iran, many store owners give customers a stick of gum instead of coins as change!

PIECES OF GUM STUCK TO THE SIDEWALK ON OXFORD STREET IN LONDON:
250,000

 THE GUM CONTINUES ITS JOURNEY BY TRAVELING MORE THAN 22 FEET (7 m) THROUGH YOUR SMALL INTESTINE.

 FINALLY, THE GUM ENDS UP IN THE TOILET, 24–72 HOURS (NOT 7 YEARS!) AFTER YOU SWALLOWED IT.

MOAI MYSTERY

A tiny island in the middle of the South Pacific Ocean is home to nearly 900 mysterious stone figures. Scattered across the coast of Easter Island, the giant statues have fascinated visitors for centuries. Who built them—and how? Read on to find out.

NUMBER OF STATUES ON EASTER ISLAND:

887

TIME TO CARVE EACH STATUE:

2 YEARS

Q: HOW DID THE ANCIENT RAPA NUI PEOPLE MOVE THESE GIANT STATUES AROUND THE ISLAND, UP TO 11 MILES (18 km) AT A TIME?

13 FEET (4 m)

AVERAGE HEIGHT:

AVERAGE WEIGHT:

14 TONS (12.7 t)

DATE CARVED:

A.D. 1100-1680

A: ROPES! RESEARCHERS WERE ABLE TO MOVE A 5-TON (4,536-kg) MOAI REPLICA MORE THAN 200 YARDS (183 m) BY ROCKING IT BACK AND FORTH.

Imagine you're an astronaut heading out on an intergalactic adventure. You're hopping from planet to planet, sightseeing across the solar system. Here's how much a 65-pound (29-kg) kid would weigh on different planets:

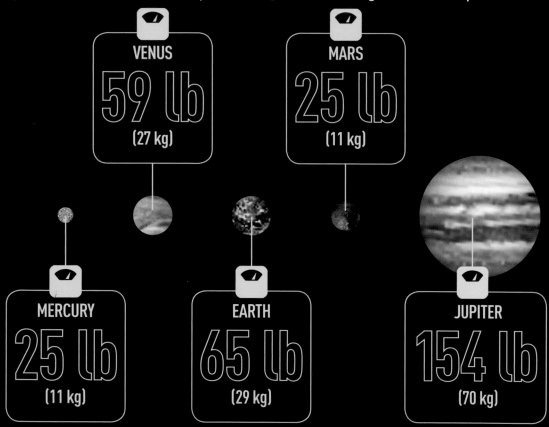

VENUS

59 lb

(27 kg)

MARS

25 lb

(11 kg)

MERCURY

25 lb

(11 kg)

EARTH

65 lb

(29 kg)

JUPITER

154 lb

(70 kg)

WHY THE WEIGHT CHANGE?

Your weight is a measure of the **pull of gravity** between you and the planet you're standing on. As you travel to different planets, the force of gravity changes depending on the planet's mass. **That means your weight changes, too!**

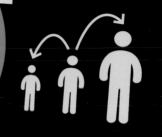

SATURN

69 lb
(31 kg)

URANUS

58 lb
(26 kg)

NEPTUNE

73 lb
(33 kg)

PLUTO

4 lb
(2 kg)

SURNAME GAME

What's in a last name? A lot of history! Geographers mapped out the most common last names across the United States and uncovered clues about the different people who have immigrated to America. Explore this map to learn about the origin of these common names.

SPANISH NAMES NEAR THE U.S.-MEXICO BORDER SHOW A LARGE LATIN AMERICAN POPULATION. **17%** OF THE U.S. IS HISPANIC.

ALASKA

HAWAII

WHERE'S THAT NAME FROM?

GERMAN AND SCANDINAVIAN FARMERS SETTLED IN THE UPPER MIDWEST.

IRELAND'S POTATO FAMINE IN THE MID-1800s SENT 1.5 MILLION PEOPLE TO THE U.S.

MANY OF THESE NAMES CAME FROM GREAT BRITAIN, SINCE THE BRITISH HAD A HEAD START ON SETTLERS FROM OTHER COUNTRIES.

SOUTH FLORIDA HAS A LARGE CUBAN POPULATION. 12.3% OF MIAMI'S POPULATION IS FROM CUBA.

LOUISIANA'S POPULAR NAMES POINT TO FRENCH AND SPANISH ROOTS.

Europe
- England
- France
- Germany
- Ireland
- Scandinavia
- Scotland
- Spain
- Wales

Asia
- China
- Japan

- Other

HOW MANY PEOPLE HAVE EACH NAME?

Smith	Fewer than 10,000
Smith	10,000 - 24,999
Smith	25,000 - 49,999
Smith	50,000 - 74,999
Smith	75,000 - 99,999
Smith	100,000 - 125,000
Smith	More than 125,000

CRAZY FOR **CANDY CORN**

These yellow, orange, and white striped kernels are a Halloween favorite. People love it so much that more than 35 million pounds (16 million kg) of candy corn is made every year! Grab a handful and find out how other people eat this century-old candy.

How Do You Eat Your Candy Corn?

11%
START AT THE WIDE END

47%
EAT THE WHOLE KERNEL AT ONCE

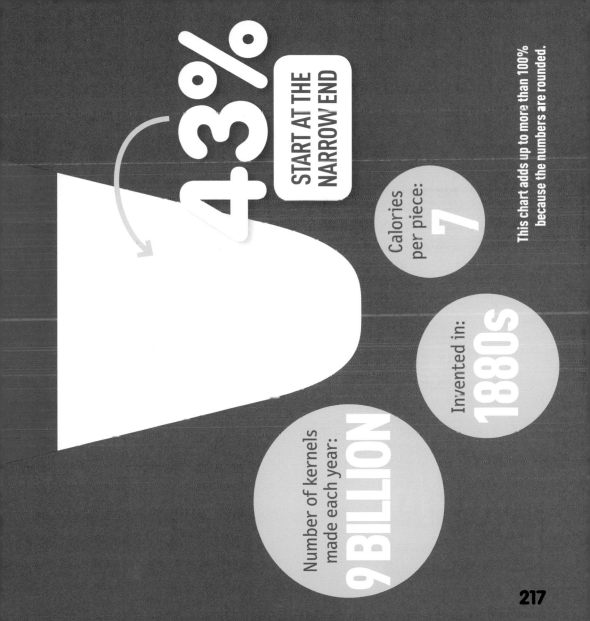

43%

START AT THE NARROW END

Calories per piece: **7**

Invented in: **1880s**

Number of kernels made each year: **9 BILLION**

This chart adds up to more than 100% because the numbers are rounded.

WASTE ROUNDUP

Each year, we create lots of waste—251 million tons (228 million t), **to be exact!** When we put glass, metal, and plastic in the garbage, it ends up in landfills, where it takes years (even decades) to decompose. Did you know that more than 70 percent of the things we throw away could be recycled instead? Take a look at these commonly discarded materials and think about what you could recycle!

14% YARD TRIMMINGS

15% FOOD WASTE

27%

PAPER & PAPERBOARD

13%
PLASTIC

9%
METAL

9%
TEXTILES

6%
WOOD

5%
GLASS

FANTASTIC **FORTUNES**

Chinese food is delicious, but the sweet treat at the end is even better. Crack open a cookie and check out these fortune facts!

You might eat fortune cookies at your favorite Chinese restaurant, but these treats are all-American! Modern fortune cookies were invented in California in the early **1900s** and are rarely eaten outside of the U.S.

Approximately
3 BILLION
fortune cookies are made each year.

That's
1 COOKIE
made for every
2 PEOPLE
on the planet every year!

There are
107
CALORIES
in a fortune cookie.

Fortune cookie dough is mixed up and baked for
3.5 MINUTES
before being folded into its signature shape.

A factory in Brooklyn, New York, makes more than **4.5 MILLION** fortune cookies per day!

NAIL NUMBERS

You've had nails for your entire life.
In fact, your nails started growing before you were born! Here's how slowly your nails grow.

FINGERNAILS GROW

.14 INCH (3.47 mm)

PER MONTH

It would take

6 MONTHS to grow an entire fingernail.

TOENAILS GROW

.06 INCH
(1.52 mm)

PER MONTH

Nails evolved from claws **55 MILLION** years ago.

SLEEPY CREATURES

Humans, birds, and even fruit flies agree: There's nothing like a good night's sleep. Here's how different animals snooze through the night—and sometimes into the day, too!

Big cats like lions sleep the same amount as pet cats:

12-16 HOURS
per day.

Newborn babies sleep up to

18 HOURS
each day.

Koalas can sleep up to

22 HOURS
per day.

Ants sleep more than 250 times a day, napping for just

1 MINUTE
at a time.

Little brown bats sleep upside down for up to **20 HOURS** straight.

Giraffes sleep just per night.

A desert snail can snooze for

SCALY STATS

This unique animal sure knows how to play defense!
Also called a scaly anteater, the pangolin is covered in sharp,
strong scales. When the pangolin is scared, it curls up into
an armored ball that is strong enough to withstand
attacks by lions. Get ready to meet one of the
strangest (and coolest!) creatures on Earth!

A PANGOLIN'S SCALES MAKE UP

20%

OF ITS TOTAL WEIGHT AND ARE
SHARP ENOUGH TO CUT ITS
PREDATORS.

THE PANGOLIN'S STICKY TONGUE CAN MEASURE UP TO

16 INCHES (41 cm)—
THAT'S LONGER THAN ITS ENTIRE BODY!

THERE ARE A TOTAL OF

8 SPECIES

OF PANGOLIN WORLDWIDE: 4 IN AFRICA AND 4 IN ASIA.

A SINGLE PANGOLIN CAN EAT UP TO

70 MILLION

INSECTS PER YEAR.

THE LARGEST PANGOLIN WEIGHED

73 POUNDS (33 kg).

THE SMALLEST PANGOLIN WEIGHED ABOUT

6 POUNDS (3 kg).

MARINE MARVELS

The marine protected areas of the United States are home to the country's most spectacular reefs, underwater ruins, and diving sites. Dive into America's most fascinating waters with these facts.

91.5%

Percentage of water in Channel Islands National Marine Sanctuary that is more than **100 FEET** (30 m) deep

1,000 MILES (1,600 km)

Length of Marianas Trench Marine National Monument, the largest marine protected area in the United States

The Mariana Trench itself is **5 TIMES** longer than the Grand Canyon!

7,000

Number of species that live in Papahānaumokuākea Marine National Monument, **25%** of which are unique to this area

41%
of the United States' waters are covered by marine protected areas.

100

Number of historic shipwrecks that happened in the area around Thunder Bay National Marine Sanctuary

126 MILES (200 KM)

Length of Florida Keys National Marine Sanctuary, home to the **THIRD LARGEST** living coral reef on Earth

Nearly
1,800
different marine areas are protected in the United States.

THE PLASTIC BAG PROBLEM

Every minute, about 2 million plastic bags are used around the world. That adds up to a big problem for the environment. Learn how you can be part of the solution—it's easier than you may think!

PROBLEM

MORE THAN
1 TRILLION

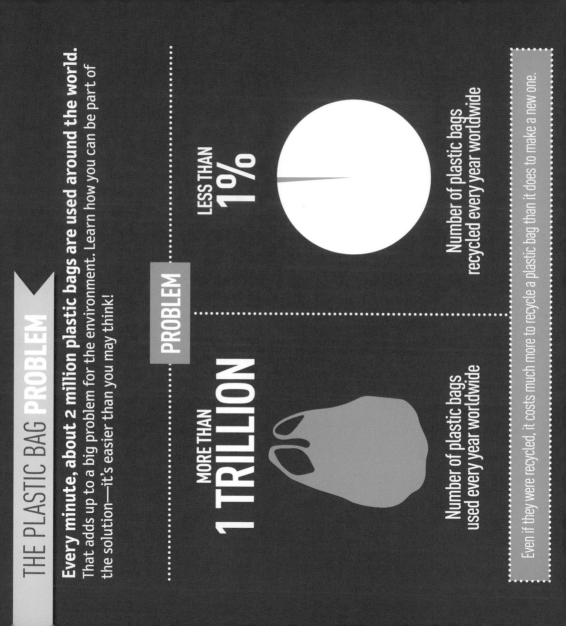

Number of plastic bags used every year worldwide

LESS THAN
1%

Number of plastic bags recycled every year worldwide

Even if they were recycled, it costs much more to recycle a plastic bag than it does to make a new one.

46,000

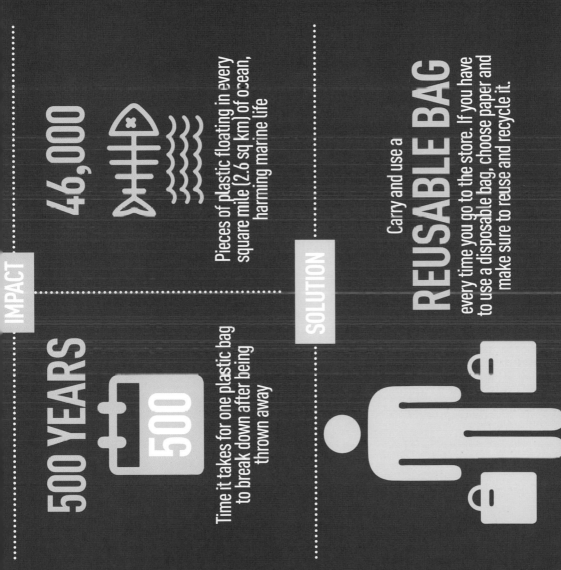

Pieces of plastic floating in every square mile (2.6 sq km) of ocean, harming marine life

500 YEARS

500

Time it takes for one plastic bag to break down after being thrown away

SOLUTION

Carry and use a

REUSABLE BAG

every time you go to the store. If you have to use a disposable bag, choose paper and make sure to reuse and recycle it.

SATELLITE STATS

It sounds like ancient history, but just 40 years ago everyone used paper maps to find their way. Today, almost anyone with a smartphone can tap into a high-tech network of satellites called the global positioning system (GPS) that can tell you your exact location on Earth. Get lost in these surprising satellite facts and use GPS to find your way home!

17
FEET (5 m)
Width of each NAVSTAR satellite

1978
The year the U.S. Air Force Space Division launched the first NAVSTAR satellite in the global positioning system

3,230
POUNDS (1,465 kg)
Maximum weight of each NAVSTAR satellite

30

Number of satellites that make up the global positioning system

4

Number of satellites needed for an accurate positioning result

8,640

MILES AN HOUR (13,905 km/h)
Speed the satellites travel around Earth, orbiting the planet twice per day

12,400

MILES (19,956 km)
Altitude at which the GPS satellites orbit Earth

How we MADE IT

An infographic may look simple and easy to read on the page, but each piece—whether it's a fact, picture, or number—needs to be carefully thought out until it looks just right. Here's how we created these cool infographics in *By the Numbers 2*.

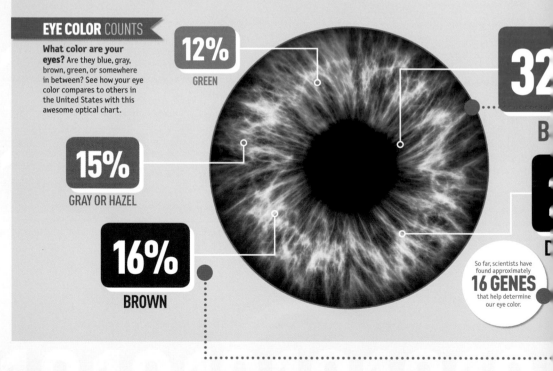

EYE COLOR COUNTS

What color are your eyes? Are they blue, gray, brown, green, or somewhere in between? See how your eye color compares to others in the United States with this awesome optical chart.

12%
GREEN

15%
GRAY OR HAZEL

16%
BROWN

32
B

So far, scientists have found approximately
16 GENES
that help determine our eye color.

First, we found a subject that was really interesting and surprising. Then our researchers looked through lots of reliable sources to find a study about eye color.

Once we have selected our subject, we can start thinking about it visually. Because these data are about eye colors, we wanted to make sure our infographic included eyes in the design. We decided to use photos to make an "eye" pie chart that helps us visualize the different eye colors.

Infographics are fun to look at, but they need to be accurate, too. Every infographic in this book was checked by a data expert. In this pie chart, each "slice" was checked to make sure that, for example, the blue eye color slice really does make up 32 percent of the whole pie chart shape.

There's so much cool information out there! We put fun facts in lots of places to show you just how amazing each infographic topic is.

Once our "eye" chart was finished, we added large numbers and helpful lines to make the chart easier to read and understand.

Create your own INFOGRAPHIC

Here's how to MAKE YOUR NUMBERS POP!

You found some interesting data. Now what should you do with all of those numbers? Instead of making a plain old pie or bar chart, make your next science or math project unforgettable with a cool information graphic (infographic)—just like the ones in this book! To make your numbers jump off the page in a fun way, check out these tips from a *National Geographic* designer. You'll be creating your own incredible infographics in no time!

EXPLORE YOUR DATA

If you didn't collect your own data, take the time to fully **understand** the numbers. Can you find any **patterns, surprises,** or **fun facts** hidden in them? If you can answer an interesting question or show a shocking surprise using your data, you'll be on your way to creating an **unforgettable infographic.**

MAKE COMPARISONS

A fascinating number fact is always interesting, but the real magic happens when you compare it to **something your audience can understand.** For example, let's say you found a source that says a family generates 6,000 pounds (2,722 kg) of trash each year. That sounds like a big number, but it's hard to visualize just how much trash that really is. When you **compare** that number to the weight of a large SUV—and show that it's the same weight—**the data really come to life!**

CHOOSE THE RIGHT STYLE

There are many different kinds of infographics, and each one is better at showing **different kinds of information.** Are you showing how something changes over time? Try a timeline! Are you comparing sizes, quantities, or values? Use a visual comparison. **Need more ideas?** Check out pages 4-5 for a guide on all the different kinds of infographics you saw in this book.

KEEP IT SIMPLE

The purpose of an infographic is to make numbers **easy to understand.** But when you're working with data, there are usually a lot of complicated numbers involved. By removing unnecessary information and showing your data in a simple way, you'll make sure anyone can understand your message.

USE A VARIETY OF VISUALS

Throughout this book, you'll not only see lots of information—or numbers—but you'll also see lots of graphics, too! This is because amazing photos and cool illustrations help the reader **visualize the numbers** we're talking about. Think about how you can use pictures to show your audience the amazing facts you've discovered.

DON'T FORGET THE DETAILS

When you're making an infographic, the little details really matter. Use labels, keys, icons, and text to help your audience understand all the facts that are relevant to your data.

MAKE IT FUN!

It's your infographic, so have fun with it! The only limit is your own creativity. Use all different **shapes** and **sizes, styles,** and **colors.** and think outside the box to grab the reader's attention. If you have fun making it, **you can bet everyone will have fun reading it!**

Want MORE?

Grab a parent and together check out these other great resources to see and learn more about infographics and design, plus awesome stats and facts.

IN PRINT

Cook, Gareth, ed. *The Best American Infographics 2015*. New York: Houghton Mifflin Harcourt, 2015.

Eaton, Thames. *The Infographic Guide to Life, the Universe and Everything*. New York: Hachette Book Group, 2014.

Heller, Steven. *Infographics Designers' Sketchbooks*. New York: Princeton Architectural Press, 2014.

McCandless, David. *Visual Miscellaneum: A Colorful Guide to the World's Most Consequential Trivia*. New York: HarperCollins Publishers, 2012.

Pease, Pamela. *Design Dossier: Graphic Design for Kids*. New York: Paintbox Press, 2010.

_____. *Design Dossier: The World of Design*. New York: Paintbox Press, 2009.

Wiedemann, Julius, ed. *Understanding the World: The Atlas of Infographics*. Cologne: Taschen, 2014.

Canva Infographic Creator

canva.com/create/infographics/

With a parent's help, try this online infographic maker that lets you experiment with hundreds of free design elements so you can make your own infographics like a pro.

Cool Infographics

coolinfographics.com

Links to the Internet's newest and coolest infographics from designers around the world, plus helpful tips and tricks you can use to make your own infographics.

Information Is Beautiful

informationisbeautiful.net

A collection of infographics about subjects like food, health, science, and technology, plus awards for the year's best infographics.

Statistic Brain Research Institute

statisticbrain.com

Want to make an infographic of your own? You'll need some interesting data! Check out this site for percentages, numbers, studies, and fascinating facts about a variety of subjects.

Venngage

venngage.com

With a parent's help, use this online tool to pick a template, add charts and visuals, and customize your own infographic.

Can You Take the Heat?
Pages 10–11
New Mexico State University. "Measuring Chile Pepper Heat." Printed February 2010. aces.nmsu.edu/pubs/_h/H237.

Pyramid Puzzler
Pages 14–15
Hekkenberg, Ans. "Ancient Egyptians Transported Pyramid Stones over Wet Sand." Phys.org, April 30, 2014, accessed February 11, 2016. phys.org/news/2014-04-ancient-egyptians-pyramid-stones-sand.html.

Dictionary Data
Pages 16–17
Fry, Edward B., and Jacqueline E. Kress. *Reading Teacher's Book of Lists*. 3rd ed. San Francisco: Jossey-Bass, 2002.

Now That's a Big Pie!
Pages 26–27
Guinness Book of World Records. "Largest Pizza." guinnessworldrecords.com/world-records/largest-pizza.

Basketball Numbers
Pages 30–31
Naismith, James. *Basketball: Its Origin and Development*. Lincoln: Bison Books, 1996.

National Basketball Association. "All Time League Leaders." stats.nba.com/leaders/alltime.

Speedy Swimmers
Pages 32–33
Froese, R., and D. Pauly, eds. "FishBase." Updated version October 2015. fishbase.org.

Olympic.org: Official Website of the Olympic Movement. "Michael Phelps Wins 7th Gold Title by a Finger Tip." olympic.org/videos/michael-phelps-wins-7th-gold-title-by-a-finger-tip.

Pushing Play on YouTube
Pages 34–35
YouTube. "YouTube Statistics." youtube.com/yt/press/statistics.html.

Fast-Food Facts
Pages 38–39
Sutter Health, Palo Alto Medical Foundation. "Fast Food." Last reviewed October 2013. pamf.org/teen/health/nutrition/fastfood.html.

Calorie averages calculated from nutrition fact data sourced from fastfoodnutrition.org.

Flusher Figures
Pages 46–47
Pritchard, Charlotte. "Is the Toilet Seat Really the Dirtiest Place in the Home?" BBC News, November 17, 2012. http://www.bbc.com/news/magazine-20324304.

Flores, Gilberto E., Scott T. Bates, Dan Knights, Christian L. Lauber, Jesse Stombaugh, Rob Knight, and Noah Fierer. "Microbial Biogeography of Public Restroom Surfaces." *PLoS ONE* 6, no. 11 (2011): e28132. doi:10.1371/journal.pone.0028132. http://journals.plos.org/plosone/article?id=10.1371/journal.pone.0028132.

Borchgrevink, Carl P., JaeMin Cha, and SeungHyun Kim. "Hand Washing Practices in a College Town Environment." *Journal of Environmental Health* 75, no. 8 (2013): 18–24. msutoday.msu.edu/_/pdf/assets/2013/hand-washing-study.pdf.

Fun Firework Facts
Pages 48–49
American Pyrotechnics Association. "U.S. Fireworks Consumption Figures 2000–2014." americanpyro.com/assets/docs/FactsandFigures/fireworks%20consump.%20figures%202000-14.pdf.

Speed Racer
Pages 50–51
Guinness Book of World Records. "Land Speed: Fastest Car." guinnessworldrecords.com/world-records/land-speed-(fastest-car).

Duran, Adam, and Kevin Walkowicz. "A Statistical Characterization of School Bus Drive Cycles Collected via Onboard Logging Systems." *SAE International Journal of Commercial Vehicles* 6, no. 2 (2013). nrel.gov/docs/fy14osti/60068.pdf.

The Scoop on Ice Cream
Pages 56–57
International Dairy Foods Association. "Ice Cream Sales & Trends." idfa.org/news-views/media-kits/ice-cream/ice-cream-sales-trends.

Inflation dollar amount calculated using measuring worth.com/uscompare.

Big Spenders
Pages 64–65
T. Rowe Price. "7th Annual Parents, Kids, and Money Survey." March 2015. corporate.troweprice.com/Money-Confident-Kids/images/emk/2015-PKM-Report-2015-FINAL.pdf.

Dollar Details
Pages 68–69
U.S. Department of the Treasury. "Bureau of Engraving and Printing Frequently Asked Questions." moneyfactory.gov/resources/faqs.html.

Tons of Trash
Pages 72–73
Duke University Center for Sustainability and Commerce. "How Much Do We Waste Daily?" center.sustainability.duke.edu/resources/green-facts-consumers/how-much-do-we-waste-daily.

Surprising Sports Stats
Pages 74–75
Kelley, Bruce, and Carl Carchia. "Hey, Data Data—Swing!" ESPN, July 16, 2013, accessed February 11, 2016. espn.go.com/espn/story/_/id/9469252/hidden-demographics-youth-sports-espn-magazine.

Bubble Buster
Pages 78–79
Sealed Air. "Bubble Wrap® 'Pop' Poll Finds Nation More Likely to 'Pop' Than One Year Ago." January 30, 2012. multivu.prnewswire.com/mnr/sealedair/48534.

You've Got Mail
Pages 82–83
United States Postal Service. "About." Information based on Fiscal Year 2014 data. about.usps.com/who-we-are/postal-facts/size-scope.htm.

Technology Top Ten
Pages 86–87
Consumer Technology Association. "Owning Innovation: CEA Study Shows Major Shifts in the Technology We Own." May 11, 2015. ce.org/News/News-Releases/Press-Releases/2015-Press-Releases/Owning-Innovation-CEA-Study-Shows-Major-Shifts-in.aspx.

Where Do Americans Live?
Pages 88–89
Map data: This product was made utilizing the LandScan (2012)™ High Resolution global Population Data Set copyrighted by UT-Battelle, LLC, operator of Oak Ridge National Laboratory under Contract No. DE-AC05-00OR22725 with the United States Department of Energy. The United States Government has certain rights in this Data Set. Neither UT-BATTELLE, LLC nor the United States Department of Energy,

nor any of their employees, makes any warranty, express or implied, or assumes any legal liability or responsibility for the accuracy, completeness, or usefulness of the data set.

A Crunchy Lunch
Pages 90–91
Van Huis, Arnold, Joost Van Itterbeeck, Harmke Klunder, Esther Mertens, Afton Halloran, Giulia Muir, and Paul Vantomme. "Nutritional Value of Insects for Human Consumption." Edible Insects: Future Prospects for Food and Feed Security (FAO Forestry Paper 171). Food and Agriculture Organization of the United Nations. 2013. fao.org/docrep/018/i3253e/i3253e06.pdf.

Time for a Vacation
Page 93
Top Vacation Spots data from American Express. "May Spending and Saving Tracker: 2012 Summer Vacation Plans." Prepared by Echo Research. April 2012. preview.thenewsmarket.com/Previews/AEXP/DocumentAssets/237764_v2.pdf

Counting at the Car Wash
Pages 94–95
Brown, Chris. "Water Use in the Professional Car Wash Industry." International Carwash Association, September 2002. carwash.org/docs/default-document-library/Water-Use-in-the-Professional-Car-Wash-Industry.pdf.

Statistic Brain Research Institute. "Car Wash Industry Statistics." Source: MSSP, IRS, Professional Carwashing and Detailing, and U.S. Census Bureau. February 2, 2015. statistic-brain.com/car-wash-car-detail-industry-stats.

Straight-A Studiers
Pages 96–97
MetLife, Inc. "MetLife Survey of the American Teacher." Prepared by Youth and Education Research. November 2007. files.eric.ed.gov/fulltext/ED500012.pdf.

University of Michigan Institute for Social Research. "Changing Times of American Youth, 1981–2003. November 2004. ns.umich.edu/Releases/2004/Nov04/teen_time_report.pdf.

Special Species
Pages 102–103
International Union for Conservation of Nature and Natural Resources. "The IUCN Red List of Threatened Species." 2015. iucnredlist.org.

Museums or Sports?
Pages 106–107
American Alliance of Museums. "Museum Facts." aam-us.org/about-museums/museum-facts.

Subject Standings
Pages 108–109
Gallup. "Gallup Youth Survey Provided by Knowledge Networks." April 22, 2003. gallup.com/poll/8248/report-card-teens-favorite-subjects.aspx.

Eye Color Counts
Pages 114–115
Statistic Brain Research Institute. "Eye Color Distribution Percentages." Source: American Academy of Ophthalmology. January 26, 2016. statisticbrain.com/eye-color-distribution-percentages.

What's Your Favorite Color?
Pages 128–129
Cohen, P. "Children's Gender and Parents' Color Preferences." Archives of Sexual Behavior 42. no. 3 (2013): 393–97 terpconnect.umd.edu/~pnc/ASB2013.pdf.

More Trees, Please!
Pages 134–135
Nilsson, Kjell, Marcus Sangster, Christos Gallis, Terry Hartig, Sjerp de Vries, Klaus Seeland, and Jasper Schipperijn, eds. Forests, Trees and Human Health. Berlin: Springer Science & Business Media, 2010.

Soil Stats
Pages 138–139
Schonbeck, Mark. "Caring for the Soil as a Living System." Virginia Association for Biological Farming Information Sheet No. 7-06. May 15, 2006. sare.org/content/download/73302/1061250/Caring_for_the_Soil_as_a_Living_System.pdf.

Nutrient Numbers
Pages 144–145
Di Noia, Jennifer. "Defining Powerhouse Fruits and Vegetables: A Nutrient Density Approach." Preventing Chronic Disease 11 (2014). cdc.gov/pcd/issues/2014/13_0390.htm/pdf/13_0390.pdf.

Game Graphs
Pages 150–151
Entertainment Software Association. "2015 Sales, Demographic and Usage Data: Essential Facts About the Computer and Video Game Industry." April 2015. theesa.com/wp-content/uploads/2015/04/ESA-Essential-Facts-2015.pdf.

Cell Count
Pages 152–153
Bianconi, E., et al. "An Estimation of the Number of Cells in the Human Body." Annals of Human Biology 40, no. 6 (2013): 471. ncbi.nlm.nih.gov/pubmed/23829164.

Man's Best Friend
Pages 158–159
Cosner, Lindsay. "The Most Popular Dog Breeds of 2014." American Kennel Club. February 26, 2015. akc.org/news/the-most-popular-breeds-of-2014.

Don't Blink!
Pages 172–173
Doughty, M. J., and T. Naase. "Further Analysis of the Human Spontaneous Eye Blink Rate by a Cluster Analysis-Based Approach to Categorize Individuals with 'Normal' Versus 'Frequent' Eye Blink Activity." Eye & Contact Lens Journal 32, no. 6 (2006): 294–99. ncbi.nlm.nih.gov/pubmed/17099391.

World Record Weather
Pages 174–175
Arizona State University World Meteorological Organization. "World Weather / Climate Extremes Archive." wmo.asu.edu.

Yummy Yogurt
Pages 188–189
Boynton, Robert D., and Andrew M. Novakovic. "Industry Evaluations of the Status and Prospects for the Burgeoning New York Greek-style Yogurt Industry." Program on Dairy Markets and Policy Research Paper No. RP13-01. October 2013. dairymarkets.org/PubPod/Pubs/RP13-01.pdf.

Happy Birthday to You
Pages 194–195
New York Times. "How Common Is Your Birthday?" December 19, 2006, accessed February 11, 2016. nytimes.com/2006/12/19/business/20leonhardt-table.html.

Surname Game
Pages 214–215
Map: Mina Liu, Oliver Uberti, NGM Staff. Data: James Cheshire, Paul Longley, and Pablo Mateos, University College London.

Waste Roundup
Pages 218–219
United States Environmental Protection Agency. "Advancing Sustainable Materials Management: Facts and Figures." Last updated December 16, 2015. epa.gov/osw/nonhaz/municipal/pubs/2012_msw_fs.pdf.

INDEX

Boldface indicates illustrations.

PHOTO CREDITS

Cover (LE), Pete Saloutos/Shutterstock; (RT), Andy Rouse/Getty Images; Back cover (LE), Vassilis Anastasiou/Dreamstime; (RT), Iakov Filimonov/Dreamstime; 2 (CTR), Andy Rouse/Getty Images; 6 (CTR), arlindo71/iStockphoto; 8 (LO LE), Madlen/Shutterstock; 8 (CTR), spauln/iStockphoto; 8 (CTR RT), Amenic181/Shutterstock; 8-9 (White Plates), Ilya Akinshin/Shutterstock; 10 (LO LE), Sompop Pundrikabha/Dreamstime; 10 (LO LE), Norgal/Dreamstime; 10 (LO RT), Eric Krouse/Dreamstime; 10 (LO RT), Jennifer Barrow/Dreamstime; 11 (LO LE), Daryl Kessler/Dreamstime; 11 (LO CTR), Eric Krouse/Dreamstime; 11 (LO RT), Adrianam13/Dreamstime; 14-15 (Bckgrd), WitR/Shutterstock; 16-17 (Bckgrd), Aopsan/Dreamstime; 18 (UP), Andrey Pavlov/Dreamstime; 18 (UP), Eric Isselee/Shutterstock; 18 (UP), Isselee/Dreamstime; 18 (UP), Andrey Pavlov/Dreamstime; 18 (UP), Isselee/Dreamstime; 18 (UP), JDCarballo/Shutterstock; 18 (UP), Tea Maeklong/Shutterstock; 18 (UP), Photodeti/Dreamstime; 18 (UP), Amwu/iStockphoto; 18 (UP), Andrey Starostin/Shutterstock; 20-21 (Bckgrd), Vadim Sadovski/Shutterstock; 24 (LO RT), Cosmin Manci/Shutterstock; 24 (UP LE), Dimijana/Shutterstock; 25 (UP LE), Melinda Fawver/Dreamstime; 25 (LO RT), Ljacky/Dreamstime; 26-27 (LO CTR), White Rabbit83/Shutterstock; 28-29 (LE), Iakov Kalinin/Shutterstock; 32-33 (Bckgrd), Mehmetcan/Dreamstime; 34 (CTR), Photka/Shutterstock; 36 (LE), Courtesy of Carlos Ramirez; 38 (UP LE), Gena73/Shutterstock; 38-39 (CTR LE), Yvdavyd/Dreamstime; 39 (LO LE), Anton Starikov/Dreamstime; 40 (LE), Itsmejust/Shutterstock; 41 (RT), Itsmejust/Shutterstock; 42-43 (Bckgrd), Irina Bg/Shutterstock; 44-45, Gerald Marella/Dreamstime; 46-47 (CTR), Aguirre_mar/Dreamstime; 48-49 (LE), Terry Why/Getty Images; 54-55 (Bckgrd), Alexander Marushin/Shutterstock; 56-57 (Ice Cream Cones), M. Unal Ozmen/Shutterstock; 57 (UP RT), Dreamstime; 57 (UP RT), Prapass Wannapinij/Dreamstime; 58 (LE), DiversityStudio1/Dreamstime; 60-61 (Bckgrd), Mircea Costina/Dreamstime; 66 (CTR), Jay Ondreicka/Shutterstock; 67 (UP LE), Isselee/Dreamstime; 67 (LO LE), Michael Adams/Dreamstime; 67 (UP RT), Frank Ellison/Dreamstime; 67 (LO RT), Anna Omelchenko/Dreamstime; 68 (CTR LE), NGS; 69 (LO RT), NGS; 70-71 (CTR), Willyam Bradberry/Shutterstock; 76-77 (Bckgrd), Cessna152/Shutterstock; 78-79 (CTR), Worker/Shutterstock; 78-79 (CTR), Gradts/Dreamstime; 80 (LO LE), Yevgeniy11/Shutterstock; 80-81 (eggs), Rangizzz/Shutterstock; 82-83 (LE), Silhouette Lover/Shutterstock; 83 (LO RT), Irinacria Photo/Shutterstock; 84 (LE), Courtesy of Rachel Binx; 90-91 (LO LE), Hurst Photo/Shutterstock; 90 (LO RT), Melinda Fawver/Shutterstock; 90 (UP RT), Le Do/Shutterstock; 90-91 (Bckgrd), Jiri Hera/Shutterstock; 91 (LO LE), Skynetphoto/Dreamstime; 91 (RT), Melica/Shutterstock; 91 (UP LE), Tischenko Irina/Shutterstock; 92 (LO CTR), NGS; 92 (LO LE), Girishhc/Dreamstime; 92-93 (Bckgrd), Aaron Lassman/Dreamstime; 97 (LO LE), Mik122/iStockphoto; 97 (UP RT), Ruslan Ivantsov/Shutterstock; 98 (UP CTR), Eric Isselee/Shutterstock; 99 (LO CTR), Thatsaphon Saengnarongrat/Dreamstime; 99 (CTR), Risteski Goce/Shutterstock; 100-101 (CTR), Hongmai2012/Dreamstime; 102 (UP RT), Tatiana Belova/Dreamstime; 102 (CTR CTR), Michael Ludwig/Dreamstime; 102 (LO LE), Amilevin/Dreamstime; 103 (LO RT), Ross Henry/Dreamstime; 103 (LO LE), Gualtiero Boffi/Dreamstime; 103 (UP LE), Lukas Blazek/Dreamstime; 103 (UP RT), Lukas Blazek/Dreamstime; 104-105 (CTR), Yevgeniy11/Shutterstock; 108 (CTR LE), Chonrawit Boonprakob/Shutterstock; 108-109 (CTR CTR), Alexan24/Dreamstime; 109 (LO RT), Vorobyeva/Shutterstock; 110 (LE), Robert Eastman/Shutterstock; 111 (UP RT), Alexsvirid/Shutterstock; 114-115 (CTR), Flowgraph/Shutterstock; 116 (UP CTR), GrigoryL/Shutterstock; 116 (CTR RT), Rmarmion/Dreamstime; 116 (CTR CTR), MarcelClemens/Shutterstock; 116 (UP RT), Pisagor/Dreamstime; 116 (LO RT), Picstudio/Dreamstime; 117 (CTR RT), Lexaarts/Shutterstock; 117 (UP RT), Somchai Som/Shutterstock; 117 (UP LE), Yobro10/Dreamstime; 117 (CTR LE), Elisabeth Burrell/Dreamstime; 117 (LO LE), Jefeatherston/Dreamstime; 118 (UP RT), Bukki88/Dreamstime; 118 (CTR CTR), Bjulien03/Dreamstime; 118 (LO RT), Galyna Andrushko/Dreamstime; 119 (LO LE), Dave Allen Photography/Dreamstime; 119 (UP LE), Terrywen412/Dreamstime; 120 (UP CTR), Carolina K. Smith M.d./Dreamstime; 121 (UP LE), Jacek Chabraszewski/Dreamstime; 122 (CTR LE), Irin-k/Shutterstock; 122 (LO LE), Gelpi JM/Shutterstock; 122 (LO RT), Loshadenok/Dreamstime; 122 (UP RT), Johanna Goodyear/Dreamstime; 122 (UP LE), Dimijana/

Since 1888, the National Geographic Society has funded more
than 12,000 research, exploration, and preservation projects
around the world. The Society receives funds from National
Geographic Partners LLC, funded in part by your purchase. A
portion of the proceeds from this book supports this vital work.

For more information, visit www.natgeo.com/info, call
1-800-647-5463, or write to the following address:

National Geographic Partners, LLC
1145 17th Street N.W.
Washington, D.C. 20036-4688 U.S.A.

Visit us online at nationalgeographic.com/books

For librarians and teachers: ngchildrensbooks.org

More for kids from National Geographic:
kids.nationalgeographic.com

For information about special discounts for bulk
purchases, please contact National Geographic Books
Special Sales: ngspecsales@ngs.org

For rights or permissions inquiries, please contact
National Geographic Books Subsidiary Rights:
ngbookrights@ngs.org

Editorial, Design, and Production by Jennifer Adrion
and Omar Noory
Art Direction by Jülide Dengel

Trade paperback ISBN: 978-1-4263-2528-1
Library Binding ISBN: 978-1-4263-2529-8

Printed in China
16/PPS/1

It all ADDS UP!

Know how to perform a card trick or wrap a gift? Do laundry or pump gas? Start a club or plan a party? From sorta silly to supersmart, get 100 helpful hints, tricks, and tips on how to be an awesome know-it-all in this fun book!